THE
IDEAL
PROBLEM SOLVER

A Series of Books in Psychology

THE
IDEAL
PROBLEM SOLVER

A GUIDE FOR IMPROVING THINKING,
LEARNING, AND CREATIVITY

JOHN D. BRANSFORD

BARRY S. STEIN

W. H. FREEMAN AND COMPANY
NEW YORK

Library of Congress Cataloging in Publication Data
Bransford, John.
  The ideal problem solver.

  (A Series of books in psychology)
  Bibliography: p.
  Includes index.
  1. Problem solving.   2. Thought and thinking.
3. Learning, Psychology of.   4. Creative ability.
I. Stein, Barry S.   II. Title.   III. Series.
BF441.B73   1984   153.4'3   84-10287
ISBN 0-7167-1668-2
ISBN 0-7167-1669-0 (pbk.)

Printed in the United States of America

1 2 3 4 5 6 7 8 9 0   SE   2 1 0 8 9 8 7 6 5 4

To
J. Ashley Bransford and her
outstanding namesakes:
Ann Bransford and
Jimmie Brown.
And to Michael, Norma, and
Eli Stein

CONTENTS

CHAPTER 6
FROM CRITICISM TO CREATIVITY   *93*

CHAPTER 7
EFFECTIVE COMMUNICATION   *109*

CHAPTER 8
CONCLUDING REMARKS   *121*

PREFACE

This book is not simply for people who love the intellectual challenge of solving problems. It is also for people who dislike problem solving or who feel intimidated by problems. And it is for people who want to help others solve problems. For example, many parents may find this book useful for helping their children perform better in school. Business leaders who recognize the importance of skills that enable their employees to identify and solve potential problems may also find this book useful. In addition, we believe that this book can provide a helpful tool for educators and researchers. For example, we have tried to illustrate how knowledge acquisition and knowledge production activities such as classroom learning and scientific research are instances of problem solving. By becoming more aware of the processes used to solve problems, people can improve their learning and their abilities to use knowledge to solve new problems that they face.

We do not claim that this book will dramatically increase your IQ, make you wealthy, or free you from all personal problems. However, based on our work with high school, college, and even graduate students, and with teachers, administrators, and business leaders, we are confident that you will find something of value that should be useful for the rest of your life. It has been our experience that different people find different parts of the book valuable, probably because people have different strengths and weaknesses with respect to problem solving. Nevertheless, we have not yet met anyone who felt that they learned nothing from this book.

A major reason for our confidence in this book is that it is solidly grounded in basic research on thinking, learning, and problem solving. Hundreds of researchers in areas such as cognitive psychology, education, philosophy, and artificial intelligence (involving problem solving by computers) have spent thousands of hours studying the processes and strategies that we discuss. We do not describe the details of these research studies because they are often quite technical. Nevertheless, references to important studies are provided throughout the book.

One of the pleasures of writing this book is that, because of our own involvement in research, we have had the opportunity to become personally acquainted with a large number of the researchers whose work provides the basis for our discussion. These researchers are some of the most dedicated, interesting, and creative people we have ever known; so it is particularly gratifying to have the opportunity to make others aware of their work. We also urge you to make use of our reference list and read as much of the original work as you can.

A number of people have asked whether we, as authors of *The IDEAL Problem Solver,* are ourselves ideal problem solvers. If you think of an ideal problem solver as someone who always knows or can immediately derive the answer to every problem, then the answer is no, we are not ideal problem solvers. As you read this book, however, you will see that our ideal problem solver is someone who continually attempts to improve by paying attention to his or her processes and by learning from any mistakes that are made. It is this *commitment* toward becoming an ideal problem solver—toward continuing to learn each day—that we endorse and try to live by. We find that it is an exciting commitment because we learn something new almost every day.

It is our hope that you too will find it valuable to think about your own problem-solving processes and that, by analyzing them, you will enjoy the continual challenge of discovering ways that they can be improved. And as you make discoveries and observations, we would love to hear from you. Your ideas will help us continue to learn.

It is impossible to thank everyone for the contributions they have made to this book. We are indebted of course to the hundreds of researchers whose work provides the basis for our discussion of learning and problem solving. In addition, some of the problems we use are classics that have been around so long that their authorship is unknown.

Some people have had such a long-term, fundamental impact on our thinking that they deserve special mention. These include Jeff Franks, Jim Jenkins, Bob Shaw, and Walter Weimer. Rick Barclay, Marcia Johnson, and Nancy McCarrell have also made significant contributions to our development. Nevertheless, none of these people should be held responsible for any of our mistakes.

During the past five or so years, we have also had the opportunity to interact at length with additional people who have made major contributions to our thinking. These include Ruth Arbitman-Smith, Ann Brown, Joe Campione, Keith Clayton, Reuven Feuerstein, Carl Haywood, and Mildrid Hoffman.

We are also grateful for the opportunity to work closely with many people who completed their graduate training at Vanderbilt—people who taught us a great deal. These include Lea Adams, Pam Auble, Sue Burns, David Chattin, Vic Delclos, Jon Doner, Joan Littlefield, Karen Mezynski, Don Morris, Greg Perfetto, and Nancy Vye. Reviews of this book by Bunny Bransford, Wesley Henry, Joy Henshall, Richard Mayer, Thomas Mosley, and Robert Sternberg have also been very helpful. In addition, we are grateful to the many students at Tennessee Technological University and Vanderbilt University who have participated in our courses on problem solving and provided us with feedback.

It would not have been possible to complete this book without the professional and cheerful help of Pat Burns and Joan Couch. They are outstanding. W. Hayward Rogers and his staff at Freeman have also done an excellent job. We are grateful to them for their work. Last but certainly not least, we thank Bunny and Jason Bransford for all their help.

John D. Bransford
Barry S. Stein

1

THE IMPORTANCE
OF PROBLEM SOLVING

The date was October 16, 1962. The President and special members of the Executive Committee of the National Security Council met in an emergency session. Information had just been obtained indicating that the Soviet Union was in the process of building missile-launching bases in Cuba. The missiles were capable of carrying nuclear warheads that could destroy most major cities in the Western Hemisphere. During 6 days of secret meetings these men had to develop a plan that would remove or destroy the missile bases before they were operational.

Several different plans were considered and evaluated. One plan called for an air strike that would quickly destroy all the missile installations. Another called for a naval blockade that might then be followed by an air strike or invasion if the missile bases were not voluntarily removed. After the blockade plan was selected, the President made a televised speech in which he conveyed details of the crisis to the nation and explained the immediate course of action that would be taken. Many historians consider the Cuban missile crisis the closest the world has come to an all-out nuclear war. Had these men selected a different course of action for the problem they confronted, the world as we know it may have changed drastically. In any case, we, the people of the world, would have had to live with the solution these men formulated, for better or for worse. Such historical events dramatically illustrate the significance of problem-solving skills.[1]

It is instructive to stop and think about the many ways in which our lives are influenced by attempts to solve problems. We studied problem solving for some time before we began to realize the following point which now seems obvious: Our lives are influenced tremendously by the solutions to problems that were proposed and implemented by people who preceded us in history. Solutions to problems like the Cuban missile crisis and polio stand out as prime examples. However, many more solutions proposed by others have an even greater impact on our daily lives. For example, you may not think of such things as stop signs, traffic signals, or rules about which side of the road to drive on as solutions to problems, but they are. Many of them were originated by William Eno, often called "the father of traffic safety." Eno, who was born in New York City in 1858, became concerned about the problem of massive traffic jams (involving horse-drawn vehicles) due to the absence of traffic regulations. Eno published an article entitled "Reform in Our Street Traffic Urgently Needed" and thereby focused people's attention on an important problem. He also proposed solutions for this problem, such as stop signs, one-way streets, and pedestrian safety islands—ideas we take for granted today.

Laws and rules represent only a small part of our everyday lives affected by other people's solutions to problems. Such artifacts as furniture, clothing, tools, and appliances are the result of additional attempts to solve problems. Even the language we speak and the number system we use are inventions that allow people to solve a variety of problems. Imagine the difficulties we would experience if we did not have a language for expressing our ideas, or if we had only a spoken language but no system for producing and interpreting written language. Similarly, consider the importance of the invention of number systems. These make it possible to solve a variety of problems that otherwise might be impossible or at least very difficult to solve.

INDIVIDUAL DIFFERENCES IN PROBLEM SOLVING

It seems clear that the world in which we live is, to a very large extent, our creation. Houses, laws, furniture, vehicles, schools, scientific theories, and books are just a few examples of things devised by humans. It is noteworthy that each of these creations or inventions was designed to solve various problems. Human beings are outstanding problem solvers, although some of us seem to be more effective at solving problems than others. Why?

One possibility is that some people are simply "smarter" than others. Another possibility is that some people have learned more than others about the processes of effective problem solving. Experimental studies show that some people are indeed more effective problem solvers than others. In addition, problem-solving abilities seem to contribute to everyday success. For example, Edwin Bliss, the author of *Getting Things Done,* got to know many congressmen in Washington, D.C.[2] and observed that the successful ones developed similar operating styles, allowing them to derive the maximum benefits from a minimum investment of time. Similarly, David Schwartz, author of *The Magic of Thinking Big,* emphasizes that successful business executives are often able to take more time off than their less successful peers, in part because they make better use of their time.[3]

Time management is just one of many areas in which successful problem solvers differ from those who are less successful. Other areas include the ability to learn effectively and to avoid blocks to creativity. We provide additional examples throughout this book.

THE TEACHING OF PROBLEM SOLVING

The important point about problem solving is *not* that some people are better at it than others. Instead, the important point is that *problem solving can be learned*. It frequently isn't learned because it isn't taught. In school, for example, we are generally taught *what* to think rather than *how* to think. This is not due to some great conspiracy to "hide the secrets of thinking and problem solving from the general public." Instead, many teachers are simply unaware of the basic processes of problem solving *even though they may unconsciously use these processes themselves*. It therefore never occurs to them to make these processes explicit and to teach them in school.

Teachers are by no means the only ones who may give problem solving less attention than it deserves. Many people do not appreciate the relevance of problem solving to their everyday activities. They often regard problem solving as a *task* students are asked to perform at the end of a chapter in a textbook or as a *process* relevant only to intellectual puzzles. However, problem solving is much more general than this.

Basically, we can say that a problem exists whenever the present situation is different from a desired situation or goal (see Figure 1.1). So, if you are at home and you need to get to work, a problem situation exists. Similarly, if you are hungry and want to eat you must solve the problem of obtaining a meal, and if you are bored you must figure out something to do. The solution to a problem involves getting from one situation to another. In the case of being at home and needing to be at work, a simple solution might be to drive your car. Generally, most people do not think of such activities as getting to work or obtaining food as involving problem solving. When problem solving is viewed in this way, it becomes clear that each of us solves a number of problems each day.

AVOIDING PROBLEMS

That we may be good at solving problems in some domains (for example, getting to work, shopping in an efficient manner, or fixing the plumbing) does not guarantee that we are also good problem solvers in other domains. Problem solving requires learning. It is quite easy for most of us to solve everyday problems, such as getting to work, because we have learned the procedures necessary for their solution. A major reason for writing this book is to show how—by becoming aware of the processes we use when solving problems successfully—we can learn to apply them to new situations. To do this, however, each of us must attempt to overcome a common tendency, the tendency to avoid problems that we cannot easily solve.

When people begin to analyze their approaches to various problems, many discover that they frequently employ a "let me out of here" approach when a problem seems difficult and an answer does not immediately come to mind. At times like this there is a natural tendency to attempt to get out of the situation and to do something with a higher probability of success.

Over time, the let me out of here approach can result in self-fulfilling prophecies. For example, people who initially have difficulty solving math problems may come to believe that they have no math ability; they may therefore avoid situations in which they must deal with math problems. Since these people receive little practice with math because they avoid it, their initial hypothesis about not being able to solve math problems is quite likely to come true. In general, it seems clear that people who avoid dealing with problems place limitations on themselves that are not necessarily there to begin with.

In our classes on problem solving we frequently present the following problem.

Imagine that the right front turn signal on your car stops working. Try to figure out why it won't work.

Figure 1.1
A problem exists when an obstacle separates the present state from the goal state.

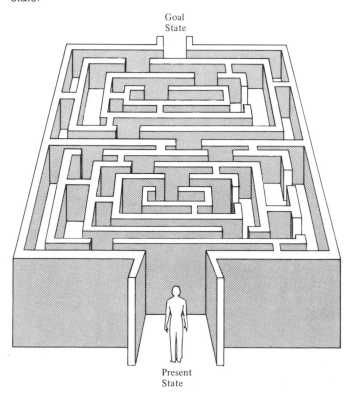

Goal
State

Present
State

For many people, the reaction to this problem is "I don't know anything about cars." They therefore assume that they cannot solve the problem. However, once they are encouraged to think about the problem, they discover that they know more than they realized. For example, a turn signal presumably requires a bulb just as a lamp does. Similarly, both a lamp and a turn signal undoubtedly require some power supply. The first step in diagnosing trouble with a turn signal might therefore be to ask whether the problem is due to the bulb or to the power supply. As a test, we could replace the bulb on the right side (the broken side) with one from the left turn signal. If the good bulb still does not work, we could then consider possible problems with the power supply—for example, a fuse may have blown. The important point is that most people can do a relatively good job of figuring out why something like a turn signal is not working *if* they think about the problem.

Negative reactions not only keep us from solving problems that we could solve, they can also keep us from exploring new areas. For example, a friend of ours became aware of ways he was limiting himself unnecessarily while participating in a weekend workshop on sports psychology. Part of the workshop was spent competing with others in such events as Indian wrestling, leg wrestling, and arm wrestling. A major goal of these activities was to help people explore their feelings about winning and losing. Since our friend was quite muscular, he won most of the events mentioned above. Nevertheless, he felt sure that he was a "humble" winner; that is, he was confident that his ego would not have been shattered had he lost.

Later in the workshop the activities turned from more "muscle-oriented" events (such as arm wrestling) to more "coordination-oriented" events. In particular, participants in the workshop were asked to learn a new type of intricate dance. As the dance instruction proceeded, our friend, who had always believed that he "couldn't dance," found that he was making many more errors than were others in the group (for example, he kept turning the wrong way.)

Our friend's most important discovery was that he had a strong reaction to his dilemma. His reaction was: "This workshop has gotten ridiculous; I'm going to leave." He almost did leave but was persuaded by the instructor to stay (the instructor was watching for such reactions and knew how to deal with them). The instructor then recruited some volunteers to work with our friend (and with several other individuals in a similar predicament) until they had mastered the dance. According to our friend, this was a very significant experience. It made him realize that he had been avoiding a number of situations because they were initially difficult. As a result of this experience, our friend resolved to increase his "courage span" when dealing with uncomfortable situations.[4]

MENTAL ESCAPES

The behavior of actually walking away from important problems is a relatively extreme negative approach to problem solving. In other cases, people may mentally "walk away" without physically removing themselves. For example, people frequently think that they are diligently trying to complete tasks, yet when prompted to stop and think about it, they realize that they have not been attending to the problem to be solved.

Consider the activity of studying a text or one's notes to prepare for a test. Most people have had the experience of going through the motions of reading and suddenly realizing that nothing has registered; attention was directed somewhere other than toward the material to be learned. Similar difficulties can arise when listening to lectures. We frequently begin to think about something else and only later realize we missed what was said.

In his classic book, *How Children Fail,* John Holt[5] emphasizes the importance of attention:

> During many of the recitation classes, when the class supposedly is working as a unit, most of the children paid very little attention to what was going on. Those who most needed to pay attention, usually paid the least. The kids who knew the answer to whatever question you were asking wanted to make sure that you knew they knew, so their hands were always waving. . . . But most of the time, when explaining, questioning, or discussing what was going on, the majority of children paid very little attention or none at all.

Holt's observations suggest that differences in attention have important effects on the degree to which people learn. He also suggests that most of us have imperfect control of our attention.

> Watching older kids study, or try to study, I saw after a while that they were not sufficiently self-aware to know when their minds had wandered off the subject.
> . . . Most of us have very imperfect control over our attention. Our minds slip away from duty before we realize that they are gone.

Lack of attention to a task is not simply a result of "disinterest" or "laziness." Attention can also be affected by fear and anxiety. For example, it can be very difficult to focus attentively on a problem while we are concerned with competing thoughts about personal problems or about fears that we may fail.

Difficulties caused by competing thoughts can be illustrated by considering a problem we presented to a number of college students. We asked them to notice their thoughts and feelings from the moment they saw the following problem. You might try this too.

> Two train stations are 50 miles apart. At 1 P.M. on Sunday a train pulls out from each of the stations and the trains start toward one another. Just as the trains pull out from the stations a hawk flies into the air in front of the first train and flies ahead to the front of the second train. When the hawk reaches the second train, it turns around and flies toward the first train. The hawk continues in this way until the trains meet. Assume that both trains travel at the speed of 25 miles per hour and that the hawk flies at a constant speed of 100 miles per hour. How many miles will the hawk have flown when the trains meet?

For a large number of the students, initial reactions to the problem included such thoughts as "Oh no, this is a mathematical word problem—I hate those things"; "Boy, am I going to look stupid"; and "I hope I don't have to turn in my answer." Furthermore, these negative thoughts frequently occurred throughout the 5 minutes allotted to the task. Such thoughts make it difficult to concentrate on problems, and indeed, despite the fact that the preceding problem requires no sophisticated math skills, a large number of the students got it wrong. (Try to solve it if you haven't done so already. The answer is presented in Appendix A.)

Fears of failure and of looking stupid are not the only activities that can interfere with attention. Frequently we all need to perform tasks (study for a test or prepare for a presentation at the office) we really don't want to perform. Under these conditions, it is not uncommon to find oneself thinking such thoughts as "I can't stand this" or "If only I didn't have to do this." As the psychologist Albert Ellis notes, such thoughts frequently involve whining.[6] In essence, we are acting like babies and whining about things "not being fair." One can continue to do this if one chooses, says Ellis. However, it is usually much more efficient to simply accept the fact that life is not always a bowl of cherries, stop whining, and get on with the task.

THE PURPOSE AND STRUCTURE OF THIS BOOK

It seems clear that simply telling people to "avoid any negative thoughts while trying to solve problems" is unlikely to produce large gains in problem-solving success. People need to know *what to do* as well as *what not to do*. Thanks to a great deal of research that has been conducted during the past 10 years or so, we now know a great deal about processes used in successful problem solving.[7] This information is frequently available only in piecemeal fashion and only in relatively technical scientific books and journals; furthermore, it is usually presented in a way that can be quite difficult to understand. Our goal is to make existing information about problem solving both comprehensible and useful. As noted earlier, we discuss such problems as learning new information and overcoming blocks to creativity. We also furnish extensive references to the scientific research that provides the basis for our discussion.

The structure of this book is as follows: In Chapter 2 we provide a model for analyzing the processes that underlie effective problem solving. The purpose of the model is to increase people's awareness of various aspects of the problem-solving process so that they can analyze their own approaches to problems. We especially emphasize the importance of viewing problems from a variety of perspectives so that creative solutions are more likely to be discovered. The model presented in Chapter 2 is used throughout the rest of the book.

As will be discussed in Chapter 2, the improvement of problem-solving skills requires that people be able to learn effectively. Just as we must learn to use physical tools (hammers or bulldozers) to solve various problems, we must also learn to use conceptual tools (strategies for remembering, concepts and theories that facilitate comprehension of patterns of data, and so on). Chapters 3 and 4 discuss ways to solve the problem of learning new information. Chapter 3 discusses techniques for improving memory. We emphasize that different types of strategies are necessary for different goals or purposes. For example, some strategies are sufficient for short-term memory but not for long-term memory. Even for long-term memory, strategies must be varied depending on the nature of the memory problem. Thus, the problem of devising strategies for remembering people's names when you see them is different from the problem of studying in a way appropriate for an essay test.

Chapter 4 discusses strategies necessary to comprehend new information. We emphasize that strategies necessary for comprehension are different from those necessary to simply memorize information. We also show why the strategies necessary for adequate comprehension are generally more difficult than those necessary to merely memorize. Nevertheless, the extra effort is worthwhile because information that is comprehended can serve as a conceptual tool for solving subsequent problems we may confront.

Chapters 5 and 6 emphasize the importance of being able to criticize ideas and to generate alternatives. These skills go beyond the ability to simply understand and remember someone else's ideas. Chapter 5 discusses strategies for spotting flaws in arguments that others may make or that we ourselves might make. These strategies are important because—whether the domain is advertising, personal conversation, or science—we are all bombarded by a host of "factual" and "logical" arguments that, when analyzed carefully, are frequently found to be full of holes.

In Chapter 6 we discuss how effective criticism can enhance creativity. People's abilities to formulate creative solutions to problems are often hampered by implicit assumptions; hence, it is important to analyze these and consider alternatives. We therefore discuss strategies for making implicit assumptions explicit and for generating a wide range of novel ideas.

Chapter 7 focuses on the topic of effective communication. A variety of strategies can help us communicate our ideas more effectively. We emphasize that different strategies are necessary, depending on *with whom* we are communicating, *how* we are communicating (orally or in writing, for example), and *what* we are trying to accomplish.

In the final chapter of this book (Chapter 8) we summarize the previous discussions and consider attitudes and strategies important for ensuring continued improvement in the ability to solve problems in a variety of domains.

NOTES

[1]For more information on the Cuban missile crisis, see R. A. Divine, *The Cuban Missile Crisis*. Chicago: Quadrangle Books, 1971.

[2]E. C. Bliss, *Getting Things Done*. New York: Bantam Books, 1976.

[3]D. Schwartz, *The Magic of Thinking Big*. New York: Cornerstone Library, 1981.

[4]R. Wertime, Students problems and "Courage spans." In J. Lockhead and J. Clements,

Eds. *Cognitive Process Instruction,* Philadelphia: The Franklin Institute Press, 1979.
    [5]J. Holt, *How Children Fail,* New York: Dell, 1964.
    [6]A. Ellis, Rational-emotive therapy. In R. Corsini (Ed.), *Current Psychotherapies.* Itasca, Ill.: Peacock, 1973, pp. 167–206.
    [7]A modern classic on problem solving is A. Newell and H. Simon, *Human Problem Solving.* Englewood Cliffs, N.J.: Prentice-Hall, 1972.

SUGGESTED READINGS

Practically Oriented Readings

S. Tobias, *Overcoming Math Anxiety.* New York: W. W. Norton, 1978.
R. L. Williams and J. D. Long, *Toward a Self-Managed Life Style.* New York: Houghton Mifflin, 1975.

Theoretically Oriented Readings

C. I. Diener and C. S. Dweck, An analysis of learned helplessness: Continuous changes in performance, strategy and achievement cognitions following failure. *Journal of Personality and Social Psychology, 36,* 451–462, 1978.
R. E. Mayer, *Thinking, Problem Solving, Cognition.* San Francisco: W. H. Freeman, 1983.

2

A MODEL FOR
IMPROVING PROBLEM SOLVING

In Chapter 1 we noted that many people have difficulty solving problems because they fail to use efficient methods. Our goal in this chapter is to provide a model that can be used to improve problem solving and decision making. The model integrates many of the contemporary ideas and research findings related to problem solving into an easily understood framework.[1] The components of the model are represented by the acronym IDEAL. Each letter in IDEAL stands for an aspect of thinking that is important for problem solving.

THE IDEAL APPROACH TO PROBLEM SOLVING

The IDEAL approach to problem solving is simple but powerful. Note that it is undoubtedly not really ideal, in the sense of being "perfect" or "the best system that could ever be created." Nevertheless, it can be extremely helpful to those who want to improve their problem-solving skills.

The IDEAL approach is designed to help you identify different parts or components of problem solving; each letter in IDEAL stands for an important component of the problem-solving and decision-making process (see Figure 2.1). Of course, actual instances of these activities do not occur in neat little compartments that are perfectly distinct from one another; the boundaries between components are usually fuzzy. Nevertheless, an exploration of the five components that comprise the IDEAL approach can be a very helpful way to become more aware of your own problem-solving processes and hence to improve your thinking and learning skills.

I = IDENTIFYING PROBLEMS

The first letter of IDEAL stands for the act of *identifying* potential problems. It may seem strange to encourage people to look for problems, but in fact, this is extremely important. These activities are overlooked in many problem-solving courses and books because the latter emphasize solutions to ready-made problems rather than focus on problem identification. This is a serious omission, because problem identification or problem finding is often the most significant part of problem solving. For example, imagine you own a business and want to know if it is running efficiently. You might hire a consultant to look for problems with your business procedures that you do not know exist.

In his book *Getting Things Done,* Bliss discusses the experiences of Marks and Spencer, a prosperous retail chain in Britain.[2] Members of that organization discovered a problem that had gone undetected for many years—too much unnecessary paperwork was required. For example, the company had a procedure for filling out cards on merchandise that was sold in order to keep track of inventory; nearly a million such cards were filled out each year. Similarly, each employee was required to fill out a daily time card indicating the number of hours worked; this again amounted to approximately a million cards each year. Within 1 year after the problem of excessive paperwork was discovered, 26 million cards and sheets of paper (120 tons worth) had been eliminated.

Ladislao Biro and his brother Georg provide another illustration of the importance of problem identification.[3] They were proofreaders and hence spent a great deal of their time checking for errors. To communicate these errors to others, they needed to write things down, of course, and it was important to write in ink because pencil often fades. However, the only way to write in ink was to use a fountain pen. Ladislao and Georg found this to be extremely messy and hence time consuming. Although you are probably not familiar with their names, you are undoubtedly familiar with their invention, the ball-point pen. The company these men created is now part of a corporation known as BIC.

A common reason for the failure to identify problems is that people do not stop to think about the possibility of improving various situations. Instead, they tend to take inconveniences and unpleasant situations for granted and assume they are simply "facts of life." Our earlier discussion of traffic congestion due to the lack of any traffic rules represents one illustration. People in the 1850s presumably did not like traffic congestion, but most did not take the time to ask whether this state of affairs signaled the existence of a problem. Until this was done, no one attempted to systematically consider how the problem might be solved.

A friend of ours recently discovered an example from his everyday life in which he had been taking something for granted rather than adopting a problem-solving approach. His experience involved the task of frying bacon. For years, he had

Figure 2.1

I	=	Identify the problem.
D	=	Define and represent the problem.
E	=	Explore possible strategies.
A	=	Act on the strategies.
L	=	Look back and evaluate the effects of your activities.

never questioned the fact that, when frying bacon, he often got splattered with grease. He simply accepted this unpleasantness as a fact of life.

One day, while looking through a mail-order catalog, our friend discovered the object illustrated in Figure 2.2. This device does an excellent job of protecting cooks from hot, splattering bacon grease. What impressed our friend most was not the invention itself, since it represented a relatively straightforward solution to the grease problem. Instead, he was impressed that someone had identified the problem in the first place. Our friend had never explicitly thought about the fact that the splattering grease signaled the existence of a problem that, if identified, might be solved.

Mail-order catalogs provide fascinating testimony to the abilities of human beings to invent things designed to solve various problems. The objects illustrated in Figure 2.3 represent just a few of our favorite inventions.[4] Note that *the first step taken by the inventors of these objects was the identification of the problems the objects were designed to solve.* Ideally, an inventor wants to identify problems shared by a large number of people. This increases the probability that the inventions will sell. (Ask yourself whether you have faced the problems that the inventions in Figure 2.3 are designed to solve.)

FAILURES TO IDENTIFY THE POSSIBILITY OF FUTURE PROBLEMS

The preceding discussion emphasized situations in which people tended to accept unpleasant situations and hence failed to ask whether these might signal the existence of a problem (or problems) that could eventually be solved. Other illustrations of the importance of problem identification involve situations in which one fails to realize that a current state of affairs may lead to problems later on. For example, for better or for worse, most countries have intelligence agencies (the CIA in the United States) that attempt to identify the existence of problems that currently exist or could soon exist. The Cuban missile crisis represents a case

Figure 2.2
An invention for reducing grease splatters.

END FEAR OF FRYING! Splatter shield keeps hot grease in, lets steam out.

in point. If the United States had failed to detect the Russian missile buildup in Cuba, Americans could have faced an immense crisis later on. On a more everyday level, people who carefully balance their checkbooks after each transaction are less likely to experience the trauma (and expense) of an overdrawn account.

Consider the following example of problem identification. Imagine that your phone rings at 3 A.M. and a man asks, "Is this Home Pac Pizza?" What should you do? If you simply say, "No, you have the wrong number," you will have failed to anticipate a problem that the caller will face as soon as he hangs up: He will not know whether he merely misdialed the number or if the number was wrong.

Several years ago, after moving and receiving a new phone number, one of us began to receive calls at all hours of the night. The callers all asked about pizza and deliveries, so there seemed to be some pattern to the calls. As it turned out, the new phone number provided by the phone company had previously been the number of an all-night pizza place.

When the calls first started coming in, we (the family members in the house) simply said, "No, you have the wrong number," and tried to go back to sleep as quickly as possible. Without fail, the phone would ring again approximately 30 seconds later and the same caller would be on the line. Since the number of the pizza place had been in the phone book (the new one had not yet been dis-

Figure 2.3
Inventions designed to solve some common problems.

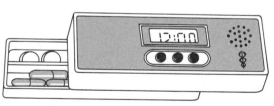

MEDICINE CLOCK. Set this little pill-box alarm to ring every ½, 1, 2, 4, 8, or 12 hours, and it plays a little song to remind you to take your medicine.

DON'T LOCK YOURSELF OUT OF HOUSE, CAR! Magnetic cases hide spare keys safely.

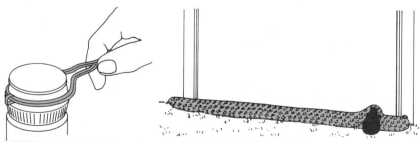

A QUICK TWIST opens the most stubborn jars and bottles!

WAGE WAR ON ENERGY COSTS. Dog sleeps in front of drafty doors and windows.

tributed), callers assumed that they had simply misdialed the number the first time around.

Once we had identified a problem with the way we answered the phone, we changed our strategy. We therefore said, "The number has been changed." The moral of the story is that it pays to look for the existence of potential problems. If problems are not identified, solutions to them are unlikely to be proposed.

$\boxed{D}$ = DEFINING PROBLEMS

The second aspect of the IDEAL approach to problem solving is defining and representing the problem as carefully as possible. We noted earlier that boundaries between various stages of problem solving are fuzzy rather than sharp; nevertheless, there are important differences between problem identification (which was just discussed) and problem definition. For example, a group of people can agree about the *existence* of a general problem yet disagree about the way in which the problem should be *defined*.

Imagine a medical doctor who realizes that such symptoms as high blood pressure signal the existence of a potential problem. The doctor has identified the existence of a problem but must still attempt to define the problem more precisely; that is, the doctor must attempt to discover the exact reasons for the patient's symptoms. Different definitions of the problem will often lead to different treatments. A patient whose high blood pressure is caused by hardening of the arteries may need different types of treatment from one whose high blood pressure is due to everyday tension from his or her job. By carefully defining the nature of the problem, the doctor has a much better chance of helping the patient find a solution that works.

Consider once again our previous discussion about frying bacon. A number of people could *identify* the existence of hot, splattering grease as signaling the existence of a problem, yet their definitions of the problem could differ. One possible definition of the problem is, "Too much heat causes grease to splatter." Here the emphasis is on the importance of heat; hence, the person's solution to the problem may focus on ways to reduce this factor. One solution is to turn down the heat on the stove (assuming that one is cooking over a stove). If the heat source is not variable (if one is cooking over a campfire, for example), the solution may be to increase the distance between the frying pan and the fire.

Another way to define the bacon problem is, "People are susceptible to burns from such liquids as bacon grease." This definition of the problem focuses on the vulnerability of people to burns. One might therefore expect that solutions would focus on ways to make people less vulnerable. A long-sleeved asbestos glove would be a good solution given such a problem definition.

A third way to define the bacon problem is "Hot grease that arises from such cooking activities as frying bacon tends to travel a relatively long way, and hence it can burn people." This definition of the problem emphasizes that hot grease splatters and can travel relatively long distances; it therefore focuses attention on ways to decrease the grease's journey. The invention illustrated earlier (see Figure

2.2) is an excellent example of a solution that might be expected to stem from such a problem definition.

THE IMPORTANCE OF CONCEPTUAL INVENTIONS

People do not simply invent objects (such as a splatter screen to protect against hot grease) that help them solve various problems. They also invent or create concepts and ideas, and these frequently reflect the ways in which various problems have been defined. The creation of units of measurement, such as *miles per gallon, passenger-miles per gallon,* and *miles per tankful* represent cases in point.

Imagine that you are a consultant for a company that wants to purchase a fleet of company vehicles to be used to get their executives to and from work. Your task is to find the most fuel-efficient way possible to reach the company's goal. One approach to the problem is to look for the type of vehicle that gets the most *miles per gallon.* Note that the problem definition here is something likc, "What is the most fuel-efficient *vehicle* that can be used to transport an executive to and from work?"

Another way to define the problem is to first focus on the number of executives who need transportation and to then determine the most effective way to do this. If many of the company's executives live close to one another, for example, one might evaluate different types of vehicles in terms of passenger-miles per gallon rather than merely miles per gallon. An emphasis on passenger-miles suggests that it may be more economical to purchase vans or even a bus.

Several years ago, when gasoline was scarce because of a severe oil shortage, many car makers focused on the concept of *miles per tankful.* For people who had to travel long distances with no assurance of finding a gas station, the unit of miles per tankful was more relevant than miles per gallon. Their definition of the most pressing gasoline problem was not, "Which vehicle permits me to go the most miles on the fewest gallons?" Instead, the major problem was, "Which vehicle will allow me to go the greatest distance without having to stop for gas?"

Remember our earlier discussion of the Home Pac Pizza problem? When we quickly told callers, "The number has been changed," they did not call back. Note that this approach to answering the phone solved only the problem of keeping people from calling back. It did not solve the larger problem of keeping them from calling in the first place. If one defines this larger problem as, "How can I keep these callers from awakening me at night?," the solution might be to take the phone off the hook. If the problem is defined as, "How can I keep people from attempting to call in the first place?", the best solution is to contact the phone company and get your number changed. (We did this, but it took time for them to make the change.)

There is another way to think about the pizza problem that involves a problem definition quite different from those discussed previously. Here, one might define the problem as, "What must I do to make use of this golden opportunity?" The solution to this definition of the problem might be to make pizzas (or buy frozen ones) and deliver them to the people who call (preferably with a healthy profit margin, of course).

REPRESENTATION AND MEMORY LIMITATIONS

In the previous examples it was easy to define the problem without experiencing a strain on short-term memory capacity. However, as the problems we work on increase in complexity it becomes more and more difficult to keep track of all the information relevant to the definition of a problem. Indeed, in some situations the procedures necessary to keep track of all the information relevant to a problem's definition become the most difficult task. Assume, for example, that you are confronted with the task of operating a large corporation or even managing a small business inventory. People responsible for such tasks frequently rely on computers, charts, and graphs to help them represent all the information relevant to purchasing and management decisions. Without these aids, they could not keep track of the problem they are working on.

Of course, one does not have to attempt to operate a business to experience the difficulty of keeping track of information. Experienced problem solvers frequently keep track of information by creating external representations. That is, rather than simply trying to keep all the information in their heads, they move it into the "outside world," they put it on paper, for example, so they can think more freely about the problem they are trying to solve.

As an illustration, try the following problem.[5]

> There are 3 separate, equally sized boxes, and inside each box there are 2 separate, small boxes, and inside each of the small boxes there are 4 even smaller boxes. How many boxes are there altogether?

Many people quickly realize the need to represent the problem by drawing, but many others do not. We know college students who attempted to do this problem in their heads and had difficulty with it. Younger students with whom we have worked (fourth and fifth graders) were especially likely to try to do the problem in their heads. Performance improved considerably when the students were prompted to draw a representation of the problem (although there is still one aspect of the problem that is easy to overlook, even after the problem is drawn out). (The answer to this problem appears in Appendix B.)

Here is another problem that requires an externalization of memory (although that's not all it requires).

> A man had four chains, each three links long. He wanted to join the four chains into a single, closed chain. Having a link opened cost 2 cents and having a link closed cost 3 cents. The man had his chains joined into a closed chain for 15 cents. How did he do it?

By actually drawing the four chains, you don't have to use memory capacity to keep imagining them. The answer to the problem appears in Appendix B.

There are many other ways of externalizing memory to keep track of information in problems. Additional examples, such as the use of graphs and Venn diagrams, are discussed later on. For present purposes, the most important point is that problems can often be defined or represented in a variety of ways, yet some representations are more likely to lead to efficient solutions than are others. For example, if you are asked, "What is ⅔ of ½?" you might represent it on paper as ⅔ × ½. A simpler way to represent the problem is, "What is ½ of ⅔?"

E = EXPLORING ALTERNATIVE APPROACHES

The third component of the IDEAL approach to problem solving is to *explore* alternative approaches for solving your problem. This involves an analysis of how you are currently reacting to a problem plus a consideration of options or strategies that might be employed.

In Chapter 1 we discussed some approaches to problems that people often do not realize they are taking. These approaches include physical escapes from problem situations (the "let me out of here" approach), as well as mental escapes in which one avoids problems by thinking of something else. However, even when people explicitly try to solve problems they often fail to use appropriate strategies. This is because, in part, some people seem to be unaware of the importance of taking strategic approaches to problems. In other cases people may be aware of the *general* importance of strategies yet may not have learned the specific strategies needed for a problem they are trying to solve.

THE IMPORTANCE OF SYSTEMATIC ANALYSIS

Consider first the general process of analyzing problems in a systematic fashion. When we watch others solve problems we cannot observe what goes on in their heads. It is therefore easy to assume that their answers just "came to them" and that, if answers don't just come to us, there is nothing we can do.

Of course, there are times when answers *do* seem to simply pop into one's mind. If you are asked, "What's 2 times 2?", for example, you simply say, "4"; the answer is overlearned. However, consider the following problem.[6]

What day follows the day before yesterday if 2 days from now will be Sunday?

Researchers have asked people who were good at problems like these to think aloud as they solved them. In no case did people simply read the problem and then have the answer pop into their minds. Instead, these experienced problem solvers took a very careful, systematic approach. In particular, they usually broke complex problems into simpler ones that could each be solved. Given the problem just presented, for example, effective problem solvers might ask themselves:

1. What is today if 2 days from now will be Sunday? (Friday)
2. If today is Friday, what is the day before yesterday? (Wednesday)
3. What day follows Wednesday? (Thursday)

The problem becomes quite simple when broken into its component parts. Furthermore, human beings seem to *need* to break complex problems into component parts in order to succeed.

The process of proceeding systematically is also necessary for effective reading comprehension. Whimbey provides information relevant to this point.[7] He presented the following passage to college students who had comprehension difficulties.

> If a serious literary critic were to write a favorable, full-length review of How Could I Tell Mother She Frightened My Boyfriends Away, Grace Plumbuster's new story, his startled readers would assume that he had gone mad, or that Grace Plumbuster was his editor's wife.

Whimbey notes that the college students who were "poor comprehenders" failed to take a systematic approach to the problem. He states:

> This was the first sentence of a reading comprehension article, and I had to stop for a moment and reread a portion of it in order to understand its meaning completely. Not so for the low-aptitude student I was testing. He was halfway down the page by the time I had the details of the first sentence sorted out. I asked him if he understood the sentence, and he answered "No, not really." So I suggested he give it another try.

Whimbey goes on to note that good readers are much more systematic in their efforts to comprehend information.

> To the poor reader, however, the pattern of gradual, sequential construction of exact meaning is totally foreign. One-shot thinking (Bereiter and Englemann's term) is the basis on which the poor reader makes interpretations and draws conclusions.

GENERAL STRATEGIES

In addition to working systematically and breaking a problem into parts, good problem solvers rely on other general strategies to help them achieve their goals. Working a problem backward is one such strategy. In many situations a problem can be worked backward more easily than it can be worked forward. For example, imagine that you have to meet someone for lunch at a restaurant across town and you do not want to be late. It is much easier to solve the problem of determining when to leave by working backward than by working forward. Thus, if you wanted to arrive at noon and you determined it would take 30 minutes to get to the restaurant, the problem could easily be solved by working backward in time (12 A.M. − 30 minutes = 11:30 A.M. departure). Generally speaking, working backward is a good strategy to use whenever the end or goal state of a problem is clear and the beginning state is not clear.

Consider the following problem (see Appendix B for the answer).

It is 4 P.M. and you have just received notification that you are expected for an important company meeting in Chicago at 8 A.M. the next morning. There are two flights open. One is a dinner flight that leaves at 6 P.M. and arrives in Chicago at 6 A.M. the next day. The other flight departs at 7:30 P.M. and arrives in Chicago at 7:30 A.M. the next day. When you arrive in Chicago you will need to wait 20 minutes for your luggage and it will take 20 minutes by taxi to get to your meeting. Which flight should you take, and will you need to buy dinner?

Another general problem-solving strategy that good problem solvers often use is to work out a complex or abstract problem by focusing on a simpler, specific situation.[8] Building scaled models or performing experiments that simulate certain characteristics of a real-world environment are good examples of this strategy. Consider the following problem (see Appendix B for the answer).

You are the director for an upcoming racquetball tournament, and 103 people have entered the open single-elimination tournament (after losing once, the player is eliminated). If you need a score card for each match, how many cards will you need if each player shows up? *Hint:* Work the problem out for a very simple case first.

THE SEARCH FOR CONCEPTUAL TOOLS

So far, our discussion of the *explore* phase of IDEAL has emphasized such strategies as breaking a problem into parts, working backward, and using a specific case. These are *general* strategies that are important for problem solving. Nevertheless, they are also relatively weak strategies in the sense that they provide little guarantee that problems will actually be solved.[9]

By far the most powerful approach to problem solving is to become familiar with concepts that others have invented—concepts that provide tools for conceptualizing and solving various problems. By learning concepts in algebra and geometry, for example (concepts that have been refined throughout the centuries), it becomes possible to solve a variety of problems that otherwise would be extremely difficult if not impossible to solve. Similarly, concepts in physics enable people to solve such problems as putting a satellite into orbit at a particular distance from the earth, and concepts in biology allow us to solve such problems as alleviating various infectious diseases. All areas of study, including biology, psychology, economics, physics, and chemistry, involve a host of core concepts and theories that people have found to be helpful for conceptualizing (defining) and solving important problems. These concepts actually *simplify* the process of problem solving.

As a simple illustration of the power of concepts, consider the drawings in Figure 2.4. By prompting people to activate concepts they have already learned, one can help them conceptualize these drawings in a new manner. The first can be viewed as a bear climbing up the opposite side of a tree and the second as the Eiffel Tower viewed from the inside of an armored car. Note how one understands the drawings differently when they are viewed from these perspectives. The philosopher N. R. Hanson argues that the creation of new scientific theories fulfills an analogous function: It enables people to conceptualize events in new and previously unappreciated ways.[10]

That concepts provide tools that have powerful effects on problem solving has important implications. For present purposes, the most important point is that people who want to develop effective problem-solving skills *must become effective at learning about relevant conceptual tools*. Therefore, much of our later discussion will focus on the problem of developing more effective learning skills.

𝔸 = **ACTING ON A PLAN**

𝕃 = **LOOKING AT THE EFFECTS**

So far, we have emphasized the importance of *identifying* and *defining* problems, plus *exploring* plans or strategies for solution. Ideally, in any particular situation, we will have defined the problem adequately and selected an appropriate strategy or plan. However, we cannot really be sure about the adequacy of our problem definition and strategy selection until we *act* on the basis of them and *look* carefully to see if they work. These last two components of the IDEAL framework will be discussed together since they are so closely related.

The cannonball problem presented below provides an excellent illustration of the importance of the *act* and *look* components of problem solving. For the present, do not try to solve the entire cannonball problem. Instead, focus only on the *first step toward solution* that comes to mind. Here is the problem.

> There are 12 cannonballs. All look alike, but one is the "oddball." The oddball is either heavier or lighter than the other balls. You are supplied with a balance scale that can hold as many cannonballs as you would like on each side of the scale. The problem is, in 4 weighings (4 uses of the scale), find the oddball.

As noted earlier: Try only the first step in this problem, that is, try the first weighing, and then consider what you have found out.

Figure 2.4
Some perceptual patterns.

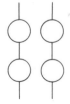
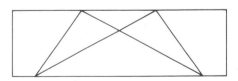

We have given this problem to approximately 100 college students. The first strategy considered by over 90% of them is to place six cannonballs on each side of the scale to determine the half that contains the oddball. Once students actively try this strategy and look at the possible effects, they discover a dilemma: They still do not know which side the oddball is on.

After their initial weighing, most students now understand the problem in a different way than they did earlier. That is, they now understand that the difficulty of the problem is related to the fact that the oddball can be *either* lighter *or* heavier; hence the, six-six weighing does not tell them which side the oddball is on. Note that, without *actively* trying their initial strategy (comparing six balls with six balls) and *looking* at the effects, the definition of oddball would not be adequately understood. (You may now want to continue to try to solve the oddball problem. The answer is in Appendix B.)

In his classic book, *How Children Fail,* John Holt describes the behaviors of children in school.[11] He notes that students frequently do not think carefully about which strategy to use when solving a problem, and once they pick one, they apply it blindly rather than actively attempt to evaluate it and look at its effects. For example, one child described by Holt was working on the following problem.

If you have 6 jugs and you want to put ⅔ of a pint of lemonade into each jug, how much lemonade will you need?

The boy's answer was 18 pints. Holt then asked the boy "How much is in each jug?" "Two-thirds of a pint," said the boy. Holt next asked whether two-thirds was more or less than a pint. "Less," said the boy. "How many jugs are there?" asked Holt. "Six," said the boy. Holt then noted that since there were six jugs and each took less than a pint, the answer eighteen did not make sense. The boy simply shrugged his shoulders and said, "Well, that's the way the system worked out." He was not used to evaluating the adequacy of the strategies he chose.

As an additional illustration of the importance of acting on the basis of plans or strategies and looking at (evaluating) the effects, consider the object illustrated in Figure 2.5. It was designed to solve the problem of reading from a cookbook while one's hands are busy with other tasks.

Assume that you are the inventor of the cookbook holder. Ideally, you would then actively try to use it and look at how well it works. If you cook like we do, you would soon discover a problem with the invention: The book is not protected from food spills and splattering grease. Given these observations, one might therefore invent the book holder illustrated in Figure 2.6. Without these observations, however, one might never discover the need to improve the invention in various ways.

As a final example of the act and look components of the IDEAL framework, imagine reading a chapter like this, and reading it only once. Assume that you understood everything as you read it. Could you therefore perform other tasks, such as list each of the problems discussed or recall each of the major points? The best way to find out is to actively attempt these activities and to assess your level of success. Many students make the mistake of assuming that they have "learned" adequately if the information seems to make sense as they read it in a textbook or hear it in a lecture. If they fail to attempt to perform such activities as recall or paraphrase, they may remain unaware of their inabilities to do so until it is too late, for example, until confronted with a test that requires such behavior. Analogously, imagine an inventor of the cookbook holder illustrated in Figure 2.6 who thinks the product is flawless until he uses it in a cooking contest and discovers, much to his horror, that his failure to provide a splatter shield results in the cookbook becoming impossible to read.

PROBLEM SOLVING AND CREATIVITY

The purpose of the preceding discussion was to illustrate five components of the problem-solving process: *Identify, Define, Explore, Act,* and *Look* at the effects. Each of these components has important effects on the degree to which problems can be solved.

In our discussion, different types of problems were used to illustrate different components. For example, the splattering bacon grease problem was used to illustrate problem identification as well as problem definition, and the cannonball problem was used to illustrate the act and look components. It is important to note that attempts to solve any problem actually involve all five components of the IDEAL framework. In addition, these attempts usually involve a number of passes through the IDEAL cycle.

Consider the problem of attempting to comprehend a passage. Assume that an effective reader is reading a text and encounters the statement, "The notes were sour because the seam split." Unlike a less effective learner who may simply be

Figure 2.5
A book holder.

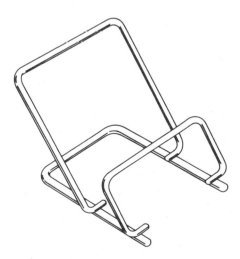

going through the motions of reading while actually daydreaming, the effective learner will realize that a problem exists (that is, he or she will *identify* the existence of a problem). Furthermore, the effective learner views the act of identifying problems as good rather than bad.

After the problem has been *identified* it must be *defined* more precisely. For example, a reader may assume that the sentence is incomprehensible because of a lack of information. The reader may also assume that her attention lapsed earlier and hence she missed crucial information in the text. This definition of the problem (or hypothesis) will lead to the *exploration* of possible solutions—an obvious one in this instance being to go back and reread the previous text. The student must therefore *act* on this idea by actually rereading and must then *look* at the effects of her activities; that is, she must evaluate whether it helped her solve the problem of understanding what the sentence means.

Assume that the act of rereading does not solve the student's comprehension problem. To the extent that she realizes this, she has again *identified* a problem. She must then *define* it, *explore* possible strategies, and so forth. In short, she has reentered the IDEAL cycle and will remain there until the problem is solved or she gives up.

Different ways of reentering the IDEAL cycle can result in strategies that are "creative" versus "less creative." The creative person who reenters the IDEAL cycle will often redefine the problem and hence try to use strategies that differ considerably from those used previously. For example, the creative problem solver may redefine the problem of failing to comprehend the sentence as, "The author left out important information." This redefinition of the problem suggests a new strategy. Rather than rereading, the optimal strategy is to generate a context that enables the

Figure 2.6
A book holder that also guards against stains.

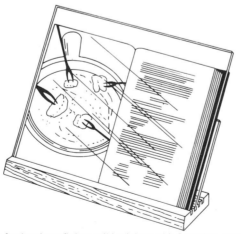

Thick Lucite pieces fit into solid oak base with 5 notches, move to accommodate any size book

sentence to make sense. (If you find yourself trying to discover such a context, the clue "bagpipes" should help.)

In his book *New Think,* de Bono distinguishes between vertical thinking (proceeding systematically from a single concept or definition) and lateral thinking (seeking alternate ways of defining or interpreting a problem).[12] He states:

> Logic is the tool that is used to dig holes deeper and bigger, to make them altogether better holes. But if the hole is in the wrong place, then no amount of improvement is going to put it in the right place. No matter how obvious this may seem to every digger, it is still easier to go on digging in the same place than to start all over again in a new place. Vertical thinking is digging the same hole deeper; lateral thinking is trying again elsewhere.

These comments suggest that an important aspect of creative problem solving is to ask yourself whether you are making implicit assumptions about the nature of a problem that are limiting your ability to find solutions.

Consider once again the four-chain problem presented earlier. The task was to connect four chains by opening and closing only a small number of links. If you solved that problem you probably had to undo a basic assumption to succeed. Initially, most people define the problem in a way that places unnecessary constraints on the situation and hence makes the problem impossible to solve—they assume that only the end links of each chain are the ones to be opened and closed. (The solution to the problem appears in Appendix B.)

Consider the following problem.

> There is a superpsychic who can predict the score of any game before it is played. Explain how this is possible.

Most people find it difficult to generate a reasonable explanation. In part, their difficulty arises because they make an assumption about the problem definition that is not necessary: They assume that the psychic predicts the *final* score of a game. If you remove this assumption, the problem becomes easier. (The answer is provided in Appendix B.)

During an afternoon seminar on problem solving that one of us was teaching, a bird flew through the room's window (which was open) and fluttered frantically around the room. There was the possibility that the bird could be injured or that people could be hurt by the bird. The teacher announced that here was a "real-world" problem to be solved. (What else could he do, given that the seminar was on problem solving?) Fortunately for the teacher, he also eventually solved the problem.

In thinking about the processes he went through, the teacher realized he did not achieve success until he had moved through the IDEAL cycle several times and had reformulated some of his initial definitions of the problem. For example, he first defined the problem as, "How can I catch the bird?" and next as, "How can I catch the bird without hurting either it or myself?" Neither of these definitions lead to a solution. Approximately 2 minutes after the bird entered the room the problem was redefined as, "How can I get the bird to leave the room?" This led to a strategy that worked on the first try (see Appendix B).

BLOCKS TO CREATIVE PROBLEM SOLVING

There are a variety of reasons people may remain locked into particular definitions of problems even though these may be unfruitful. An important reason that was discussed earlier is that people may be unaware they are making assumptions; they therefore fail to consider alternatives. Another reason is that people may be so personally involved ("ego involved") in their own approach to a particular problem that they have difficulty considering alternatives. They therefore keep trying to show they were right all along rather than attempt to find alternative ways a problem might be defined.

Scientists are individuals who frequently must attempt to think about problems from new perspectives. According to popular portrayal in the media, scientists are supposed to be "totally objective" and seek "only the truth." In actuality, scientists are much more human than this. Their humanity has both positive and negative implications. On the positive side, scientists generally make better parents, friends, and spouses than one would expect if they were totally cold hearted. On the negative side, scientists frequently have difficulty abandoning sets of assumptions that are near and dear to their hearts.

The physicist David Bohm discusses the emotional impact of receiving criticisms that question one's initial approach to an area (one's definition of a problem). He describes a scientist's reaction to alternative assumptions proposed by another scientist.[13]

> His first reaction is often of violent disturbance, as views that are very dear are questioned or thrown to the ground. Nevertheless, if he will "stay with it" rather than escape into anger and unjustified rejection of contrary ideas, he will discover that this disturbance is very beneficial. For now he becomes aware of the assumptive character of a great many previously unquestioned features of his own thinking. This does not mean that he will reject these assumptions in favor of those of other people. Rather, what is needed is the conscious criticism of one's own metaphysics, leading to changes where appropriate and ultimately, to the continual creation of new and different kinds.

Clearly, scientists are not the only people who have difficulty redefining problems because of emotional attachments to various sets of assumptions. Nearly all people experience such difficulties at some point or another. When this happens, we fail to critically evaluate our current assumptions. The IDEAL approach provides an important reminder of the value of questioning assumptions and defining problems in new ways.

SUMMARY

Our goal in this chapter was to provide a model that can be used to improve problem solving. The model, represented by the acronym IDEAL, emphasizes five components of the problem-solving process: *identify, define, explore, act,* and *look* at the effects. We noted that each of these components is involved in any attempt to solve a problem; furthermore, people must frequently move through the IDEAL cycle a number of times to arrive at a satisfactory solution. Creative problem solvers are especially likely to view a problem from a variety of perspectives; that is, to define a problem in a number of different ways.

In the remaining chapters we apply the IDEAL model to situations in which people must solve such problems as remember sets of facts, comprehend new information, spot flaws in arguments, and communicate effectively. Since the IDEAL model provides the organizing structure for the rest of this book, it is important that you understand it and be able to use it in a variety of ways. To help you reach this goal, we include at the end of this and other chapters a variety of exercises designed to provide practice at thinking in terms of the IDEAL framework. The exercises are designed to be fun as well as informative. Some include problems to solve; others involve quotations, statements of fact, and so forth. The exercises are designed to illustrate how the IDEAL framework can be used to think about a variety of situations. The best way to work with these exercises is to first read the problem or statement, think about it for a while, and then turn to the answers at the back of the book to see how we thought about it from the IDEAL perspective. Our thoughts will not be the only ones that could be correct, and they may often be less interesting than your own. Nevertheless, by seeing how we use the IDEAL approach to think about experiences, you should become able to see the world from this perspective and to evaluate for yourself whether or not it is useful.

EXERCISES

Try to solve the two following problems as quickly as possible.

1. *Quickly, now:* How many members of each species did Adam take with him on the Ark? (Note that the question is how many *members* of each species rather than how many species.) Do not look up the answer until you have also tried the problem below.

2. Spend approximately 5 seconds studying the phrases presented below, and then, without looking back at them, write down what you saw. Please begin now.

Are the inventions shown below simply gimmicks, or do they address real needs?

3. Talking scale:

4. Sound-activated light switch:

Two actual inventions are shown below. Try to define the problems they were designed to solve.

5.

6.

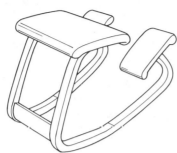

7. What kind of problems were these inventions designed to solve?

? . , !

8. Can you make sense of the following?

That that is is not that that is not is that it it is

9. One morning, exactly at sunrise, a Buddhist monk began to climb a tall mountain. The narrow path, no more than a foot or two wide, spiraled around the mountain to a glittering temple at the summit. The monk ascended the path at varying rates of speed, stopping many times along the way to rest and to eat the dried fruit he carried with him. He reached the temple shortly before sunset. After several days of fasting and meditation, he began his journey back along the same path, starting at sunrise and again walking at variable speeds with many pauses along the way. His average speed descending was, of course, greater than his average climbing speed.

Prove that there is a spot along the path that the monk will occupy on both trips at precisely the same time of day.

10. A social psychologist was interested in the custom of handshaking. He noticed that some people are more inclined than others to shake hands when they are introduced. One evening when he and his wife had joined four other couples at a party, he took advantage of the occasion to collect data. He asked each of the other nine people at the party how many people they had shaken hands with during the introductions. He received a different answer, from zero through eight, from each of the nine people. You can assume that husbands and wives don't shake hands with each other during introductions, and of course, people don't shake hands with themselves. Given this information, find out how often the psychologist's wife shook hands.*

11. There are two large jars. One jar is filled with a large number of blue beads and the other is filled with the same number of red beads. Five beads from the red bead jar are scooped out and dumped in the blue bead jar. Someone then puts a hand in the blue bead jar and scoops out five beads without knowing what color they are and dumps them into the red bead jar. Are there the same number of red beads in the red bead jar as there are blue beads in the blue bead jar?

12. In an article they wrote, Mel Mark and Thomas Cook describe the case of Shirley Smith (a fictitious name) who had become overwhelmed by a sense that her family was economically deprived. In actuality, however, Shirley's economic condition had

*From J. R. Hayes, *The Complete Problem Solver*. Philadelphia: Franklin Institute Press, 1981.

recently improved. Just 1 year before, both she and her husband had been struggling students. They lived in an apartment for married graduate students and had to work hard to make ends meet. Recently, the Smiths moved to an affluent big city suburb where Mr. Smith has a postdoctoral fellowship and is doing very well. How can one explain Shirley's increased feeling of dissatisfaction with her family's economic condition despite the fact that it has improved greatly?

13. Imagine you have a piece of tissue paper, such as a Kleenex tissue. If you fold the paper in half it doubles in thickness; if you fold it in half again it is now four layers thick. Imagine that it is possible to fold the paper a total of 50 times, and assume that the sheet of paper was originally 0.001 inch thick. How thick would the folded paper be after 50 folds?

14. Suppose that each of the fish illustrated below eats two fish in front of it each day. That is, fish 1 eats 2 like fish 2, each fish 2 eats 2 like fish 3, each fish 3 eats 2 like fish 4, and so forth. How many of fish 7 will be eaten to supply fish 1 with enough food for 1 day?

15. At the top of the next page is a design* for a robot (imaginary) manufactured to wash outside windows in high-rise buildings. It has suction-cup feet (to help it climb), a bucket head (to hold water), large sponges as hands (since the windows are large), a padded stomach (so it won't scratch the building), a battery (for power), and a parachute (in case it falls). Do you think the design is adequate?

16. Assume that a man has 25 cigar butts and that he uses 5 butts to make a new cigar (he rerolls the butts). How many cigars can he smoke after he has made them?

*From G. Teague, Constraints on Effective Illustrations. Master Thesis, Tennessee Technological University.

NOTES

[1]Examples of theoretical orientations that are related to the IDEAL framework are: A. Newell and H. A. Simon, *Human Problem Solving*. Englewood Cliffs, N.J.: Prentice-Hall, 1972; G. Polya, *How to Solve It*. Garden City, N.Y.: Doubleday Anchor, 1957; R. J. Sternberg, Intelligence as thinking and learning skills, *Educational Leadership, 39,* 18–20, 1981.

[2]E. C. Bliss, *Getting Things Done*. New York: Bantam Books, 1976.

[3]This example is from E. de Bono (Ed.), *Eureka, An Illustrated History of Inventions from the Wheel to the Computer,* London Sunday Times Encyclopedia. New York: Holt, Rinehart & Winston, 1974.

[4]Additional examples of inventions can be found in deBono (see note 3).

[5]This problem is from A. Whimbey and J. Lochhead, *Problem Solving and Comprehension: A Short Course in Analytical Reasoning*. Philadelphia: Franklin Institute Press, 1980.

[6]From Whimbey and Lochhead, 1980 (see note 5).

[7]A. Whimbey, with L. S. Whimbey, *Intelligence Can Be Taught*. New York: Dutton, 1975.

[8]Additional examples of general problem-solving strategies can be found in B. F. Anderson, *The Complete Thinker*. Englewood Cliffs, N.J.: Prentice-Hall, 1980; J. R. Hayes, *The Complete Problem Solver*. Philadelphia: Franklin Institute Press, 1981; G. Polya, *How to Solve It*. Garden City, N.Y.: Doubleday Anchor, 1957; W. A. Wickelgren, *How to Solve Problems*. San Francisco: W. H. Freeman, 1974.

[9]For an excellent discussion of general versus specific strategies and skills, see A. Newell, One final word. In D. T. Tuma and F. Reif (Eds.), *Problem Solving and Education: Issues in Teaching and Research*. Englewood Cliffs, N.J.: Prentice-Hall, 1980.

[10]N. R. Hanson, A picture theory of theory meaning. In R. G. Colodny (Ed.), *The Nature and Function of Scientific Theories*. Pittsburgh: University of Pittsburgh Press, 1970.

[11]J. Holt, *How Children Fail*. New York: Dell, 1964.

[12]E. de Bono, *New Think*. New York: Basic Books, 1967.

[13]D. Bohm, Further remarks on order. In C. H. Waddington (Ed.), *Towards a Theoretical Biology,* Vol. 2. Chicago: Aldine Press, 1969.

SUGGESTED READINGS

Practically Oriented Readings

Anderson, B. F. *The Complete Thinker*. Englewood Cliffs, N.J.: Prentice-Hall, 1980.

Hayes, J. R. *The Complete Problem Solver*. Philadelphia: Franklin Institute Press, 1981.

Polya, G. *How to Solve It*. Garden City, N.Y.: Doubleday Anchor, 1957.

Rubinstein, M. F., and K. Pfeiffer, *Concepts in Problem Solving*. Englewood Cliffs, N.J.: Prentice-Hall, 1980.

Wickelgren, W. A. *How to Solve Problems*. San Francisco: W. H. Freeman, 1974.

Theoretically Oriented Readings

Bransford, J. D., B. S. Stein, R. Arbitman-Smith, and N. J. Vye, Three approaches to teaching thinking and learning. In J. Segal, S. Chipman, and R. Glaser (Eds.), *Thinking and Learning Skills: Relating Instruction to Basic Research,* Vol. 1. Hillsdale, N.J.: Erlbaum, in press.

Humphrey, G. *Thinking: An Introduction to Its Experimental Psychology*. New York: Wiley, 1963.

Lochhead, J., and J. Clement, *Cognitive Process Instruction: Research on Teaching Thinking Skills*. Philadelphia: Franklin Institute Press, 1979.

Mandler, J. M., and G. Mandler, *Thinking: From Association to Gestalt*. New York: Wiley, 1964.

Mayer, R. E., *Thinking, Problem Solving, Cognition*. San Francisco: W. H. Freeman, 1983.

Sternberg, R. J., Intelligence and thinking and learning skills, *Educational Leadership, 39,* 18–20, 1981.

Tuma, D. T., and F. Reif (Eds.), *Problem Solving and Education: Issues in Teaching and Learning*. Hillsdale, N.J.: Erlbaum, 1980.

Wason, P. C., and P. N. Johnson-Laird, *Thinking and Reasoning*. Baltimore: Penguin, 1968.

Wertheimer, M., *Productive Thinking*. New York: Harper & Row, 1959.

3

IMPROVING MEMORY SKILLS

The unassisted hand and the understanding left to itself possess but little power. Effects are produced by means of instruments and helps, which the understanding requires no less than the hand.

Sir Francis Bacon, 1620[1]

As we noted in Chapter 2, one of the most powerful ways to improve your problem-solving abilities is to become familiar with conceptual tools that have been developed and refined throughout history. These tools include (1) strategies for representing and manipulating information (like working backward or using Venn diagrams,) and (2) core concepts that provide coherence and structure to particular areas such as physics, economics, sociology, psychology, and history. As Bacon argues, humans' abilities to perform such physical feats as moving boulders, removing trees, or lifting heavy objects are quite limited. Our powers have been increased tremendously by the invention of tools (levers, bulldozers, cranes, and saws). Like our physical powers, Bacon argues that our inherent mental powers are also quite limited. They become much stronger through the use of "instruments" and "helps," that is, through the use of appropriate conceptual tools.

The goal of this chapter is to explore strategies that can increase our abilities to remember information. These strategies (or "mental helps" as Bacon might have called them) operate like other useful tools that humans have developed. Like a good hammer, for example, a memory tool can help us perform tasks that otherwise would be difficult or perhaps even impossible to perform. However, just as a hammer may be appropriate for some tasks but not others (pounding nails versus tightening a bolt), a particular memory strategy may or may not be appropriate depending on the nature of the memory problem. The *exploration* and eventual selection of strategies must therefore be preceded by a careful *identification* and *definition* of the particular memory problem to be solved, and the appropriateness of strategies must be evaluated by *actively* applying them and *looking* at their effects. Note that these activities are all components of the IDEAL model discussed in Chapter 2. This model will provide the basis for our discussion of improving memory performance. We begin with an analysis of a simple memory task.

REMEMBERING AS PROBLEM SOLVING

Here is a memory problem to solve. The list below contains twenty-five words; spend approximately 1½ minutes studying the list (this amounts to approximately 4 seconds per word). Then, without looking at the list, write down as many of the words as you can. Please begin now.

couch potato hat trumpet boat desk carrot shirt piano cat
chair watermelon pants harp airplane table bread coat violin
bicycle bed tomato glove drum truck

People take a variety of approaches to such memory problems. We will discuss these differences from the perspective of the IDEAL approach to problem solving described in Chapter 2.

At first glance, one might assume that all people *identify* the existence of a problem since they are explicitly introduced to a problem to be solved. However, people differ in the degree to which they identify an ambiguity in the instructions for the memory problem. The instructions are to write down as many words as you can, but nothing is said about order. There are important differences between remembering words in any order and remembering them in the exact order in which they occurred.

People's responses to the ambiguity in the instructions reflect different *definitions* of the memory problem. Some assume that they must recall the words in the exact order in which they were presented; others assume that they can recall the words in any order they choose. Note that people could define the problem in a particular way without realizing the ambiguity in the instructions to the problem. Others may notice the ambiguity and then make an assumption about how the problem should be defined.

Assume that the problem is defined as, "recall the words in any order" (in fact, most people make this assumption). Even though people may agree on this definition of the problem, there are large differences in their *exploration* of possible strategies. Here are some examples of strategies that are frequently used.

1. Rehearse each word a number of times as it is read ("couch," "couch," "couch").
2. Rehearse words in groups (while reading the third word, go back and rehearse it with the second and first word).

3. Organize the words into conceptual categories (think of "couch" and "desk" as instances of furniture, "glove" and "coat" as instances of clothing, and so on).
4. Make up a story that links each of the words on the list. ("While cleaning under his *couch,* Bill found a week-old *potato.* He hid it under his *hat* when a friend came over to borrow his *trumpet.* . . .")
5. Form vivid images or "mental pictures" of objects (form an image that includes a couch, potato, hat, and so on).

We discuss various strategies in more detail later. For present purposes it is important to note that people's approaches to the preceding memory problem also differ with respect to the act and look components of the IDEAL process. For example, some people begin by *actively* trying a strategy (simple rehearsal) and *looking* at the effects ("I seem to forget what I just rehearsed"). They may therefore change strategies as they proceed through the list. In contrast, other people use the same strategy throughout the entire task. Differences in the act and look components would become even more apparent if the task were changed. For example, imagine that the problem was to study until one was confident of his or her ability to recall *all* the words on the list. Given this definition of the problem, one would expect people to actively attempt to recall the list after each study trial, to look at the effects, and to react accordingly. Effective learners would undoubtedly change their strategies if the initial ones seemed ineffective, and they would concentrate their attention on words that they could *not* recall rather than think only about those that they *could* recall.

The Effectiveness of Different Strategies

If you experiment with memory problems like the one just presented, you will undoubtedly find that some of the strategies listed above are more effective than others. For example, the simple strategy of rehearsing each word several times will usually result in poorer recall than the use of such strategies as organizing words into relevant categories or making up a story (and perhaps supplementing it with images) that links each of the words.[2] Later we discuss why some strategies are better than others.

It is important to note, however, that the appropriateness of various strategies depends on the nature of the memory problem you are trying to solve. Suppose you look up a new phone number (for example, 323–2875) and want to remember it only long enough to walk across the room to dial it. You are therefore attempting to solve a problem involving short-term memory rather than long-term memory. An effective strategy in this case is simply to rehearse the number by saying it to yourself as you walk across the room. Interestingly, even the use of this simple strategy involves a relatively sophisticated level of problem solving. For example, studies with children in kindergarten showed that, despite seeming to really *want* to remember information, many children failed to realize that they needed to rehearse the information.[3] Not surprisingly, those who did not rehearse also did not remember well.

The memory problem presented earlier in this chapter contained twenty-five words. This is far too many words to be able to hold in short-term memory by simply rehearsing them (generally, we can hold only from five to nine units of information in short-term memory).[4] The twenty-five word problem requires that we store information in long-term memory; hence, such strategies as simple rehearsal are not as effective as those that involve categorization or the construction of stories and images. Nevertheless, even these latter strategies are effective only for certain types of memory problems.

As an illustration of this argument, note once again that our earlier memory problem involved the ability to recall words *in any order you choose*. Imagine that the task had been to recall the words in their exact order of appearance. Strategies involving attempts to categorize words are not optimal for this task, whereas strategies involving the construction of stories that link each word are quite appropriate. In contrast, if the task is to state as quickly as possible the categories suggested by the words on a list, the categorization strategy is much more effective than the story strategy. Similarly, assume that the task is to recall all the words in the *reverse* order of occurrence, and to do this quickly. The categorization strategy is not appropriate, and the story strategy also leads to problems because it is difficult to tell a story from the end to its beginning (later we discuss strategies for recalling things in reverse order).

Here are some additional memory tasks that one might want to perform following exposure to a list of twenty-five words.

1. Remember the number of words that contain at least one *e*.
2. Remember the number of two-syllable words.
3. Remember the word that occurred third, fifth, tenth, and twentieth on the list.
4. Remember how many words were homonyms (have at least two distinct meanings, such as traffic jam versus strawberry jam).
5. Remember the words in alphabetical order.

Each of these tasks requires the use of different strategies during learning. Remembering therefore involves problem solving, and effective problem solvers must be flexible; they must define problems carefully and must utilize different strategies depending on the nature of the memory problem they are asked to solve.

Try the following memory problem. Study the passage below until you can remember its main points.

Many foods should not cost as much as you usually pay. Food costs would diminish if farm land was not so costly. In addition, tractors and additional tools cost way too much. Politicians should also diminish any tax on farm products. A high tax on such products hurts us all.

If you studied the passage, the chances are quite good that you can easily recall its main points. However, without looking back at the passage, suppose you are given 10 seconds to answer a different question; namely, "How many words in the passage contained the letter *e?*" You might be able to estimate the number of *e*'s by recalling the words and checking each one, but this will take a considerable amount of time and you will probably make some mistakes (most passages of this length would include a considerable number of *e*'s, but not this one). The question about *e*'s could have been answered much more easily and accurately if you had known about it *before* studying the passage. You would then have been able to use a different strategy during learning. This provides a simple illustration of how particular strategies may or may not be optimal depending on the nature of the memory problem to be solved.[5]

MEMORY AND RETRIEVAL PROCESSES

People who study human memory emphasize the differences between *storing* information and *retrieving* it.[6] The demonstration experiment presented below is designed to illustrate the importance of retrieval processes for remembering. Instructions are as follows.

Spend 3 to 5 seconds reading each of the sentences presented in the list below, and read through the list only once. As soon as you finish, remove the list from sight and write down as many of the sentences as you can. Please begin now.

A brick can be used as a doorstop.
A ladder can be used as a bookshelf.
A wine bottle can be used as a candleholder.
A pan can be used as a drum.
A record can be used to serve potato chips.
A guitar can be used as a canoe paddle.
A leaf can be used as a bookmark.
An orange can be used to play catch.
A newspaper can be used to swat flies.
A TV antenna can be used as a clothes rack.
A sheet can be used as a sail.
A boat can be used as a shelter.
A bathtub can be used as a punch bowl.
A flashlight can be used to hold water.
A rock can be used as a paperweight.
A knife can be used to stir paint.
A pen can be used as an arrow.
A barrel can be used as a chair.
A rug can be used as a bedspread.
A telephone can be used as an alarm clock.
A scissors can be used to cut grass.
A board can be used as a ruler.
A balloon can be used as a pillow.
A shoe can be used to pound nails.
A dime can be used as a screwdriver.
A lampshade can be used as a hat.

Now, recall as many of the sentences as you can. You need not write "can be used as" each time.

Most people recall between ten and sixteen sentences. For present purposes, we are interested in those sentences that were *not* recalled. What happened to them? Did you fail to encode them because of a lapse of attention? Did you attend to them, yet forget them quickly? Are they actually in memory but can't be found?

Most people who participate in the demonstration experiment are convinced that they learned *more* than they can recall. They believe that they are simply unable to find all the information that has been stored. These feelings suggest that there may be important differences between storing information and retrieving it later on.

The presentation of appropriate retrieval cues can help one find information that is stored but was not retrieved initially. Without looking back at the preceding list of sentences, read the following instructions.

The words in the list below are potential retrieval cues. They are the subjects (the first noun) of the sentences you just tried to recall. Read each cue and see if it reminds you of a sentence from the previous list. Keep track of how many sentences you now remember so that you can compare this performance to your initial attempt to remember without the help of cues. Please begin now.

flashlight	lampshade
sheet	shoe
rock	guitar
telephone	scissors
boat	leaf
dime	brick
wine bottle	knife
board	newspaper
pen	pan
balloon	barrel
ladder	rug
record	orange
TV antenna	bathtub

If you compare the first memory performance (without cues) with your performance given the help of cues, you should find a substantial increase on the second trial. Many people find that cues frequently produce an "aha" experience; cues remind them of information that was stored but not retrieved during the first recall trial. Such experiences suggest that memory not only requires storage, it requires retrieval as well.

Effects of Strategies on Retrieval

We noted earlier that, given particular memory goals, some kinds of strategies were more effective than others. An important reason for the effectiveness of various strategies is that they help people provide their own retrieval cues. For example, rehearsal strategies that actively relate different words to one another are more likely to facilitate retrieval (recall of one word acts as a cue for another) than are rehearsal strategies that simply repeat each individual word a number of times ("couch," "couch," "couch"). Strategies involving the organization of words into categories (furniture or clothing) or the organization of words into an integrated story or image also provide structures that can help people generate their own retrieval cues.

An especially important strategy for facilitating retrieval is to create an *acronym* that is easy to remember and that can remind you of important ideas. Assume, for example, that you want to remember the component processes involved in problem solving that were discussed in Chapter 2. An excellent way to do this is to think of the acronym IDEAL, which can then serve as a retrieval cue for remembering information about individual components (identify, define, explore, act, and look). Effective learners frequently create their own acronyms to remember information they need to know.

Some acronyms have become so widely used and accepted that the acronym is typically used in place of the underlying concepts or terms (such as radar—radio detecting and ranging). In practice, the use of acronyms is based on principles similar to the practice of forming abbreviations for complex terms or names. Such terms as DNA, RNA, and IQ are examples of widely used mental shorthands. It is very common for experts in a given field of study to invent their own shared language or mental shorthands by using a variety of acronyms and abbreviations. This jargon can facilitate communication between the experts but make it difficult for those outside the field to understand. In contrast, business leaders will often use acronyms and abbreviations to help the outsider or consumer remember their names or obtain their services. Some examples of these uses are:

IBM
3-M
Dial 526-film for theater information

A related strategy for remembering important terms is to think of a short phrase with words that begin with letters that represent the information to be remembered. For example, to remember the notes of the G clef, it is helpful to use the phrase "every good boy does fine." Such phrases are called *acrostics*. Both acrostics and acronyms can be effective strategies because they substitute an easily remembered word or phrase for more complex and unrelated concepts; in short, they substitute an easier memory task for a more difficult one. These strategies work as long as the letters can function as effective retrieval clues for each concept to be remembered. However, such strategies might not be very effective for remembering unfamiliar words or concepts. For example, most people would not find the word *bunt* to be a good acronym for remembering the names Baum, Ulpa, Nidia, and Treim because the names themselves have not yet been learned. Similarly, the strategy of using an acrostic would be ineffective if the acrostic itself were so complex that it could not be remembered.

IMPROVING THE EFFECTIVENESS OF RETRIEVAL CUES

In the preceding discussion we emphasized that (1) a particular memory strategy may or may not be appropriate, depending on the nature of the memory problem, and (2) people may often store information yet be unable to retrieve it. After reading the statement, "A record can be used to serve potato chips," for example, a person may store this information yet fail to retrieve it during recall. If later supplied with the cue "record," however, that person may now recall the entire sentence, often with a feeling of "of course" or "aha."

An important question is: What determines whether a retrieval cue will be effective?[7] In the preceding example, "record" was an effective retrieval cue for "can be used to serve potato chips." Nevertheless, there are many cases in which potential cues are not effective. For example, you have undoubtedly experienced many instances when, upon meeting people, you see their faces and hear their names. Ideally, when you see these people later you should remember their names because their faces act as retrieval cues. Nevertheless, many people find that they cannot recall people's names effectively. Why?

We discuss strategies for linking faces and names later in this chapter. First, it is important to get a better idea of some of the processes necessary for something to become an effective retrieval cue. In the demonstration experiment below you will see sixteen *pairs* of words. *Please simply read each word as you go through the list and try to do nothing more than this* (try to spend approximately 4 seconds per pair). After reading the list once, you will be supplied with some potential retrieval cues. Please begin now.

clock	sheep	pencil	cloud
telephone	dog	book	fence
rock	baby	stove	owl
cloud	ring	mountain	egg
rabbit	shovel	robin	flute
bear	ice cube	tent	movie
fox	lamp	key	snake
tree	radio	snow	elephant

In the list below you will receive the first member of each of the sixteen pairs of words you just read. When you read each word, try to think of the second word that went with it, but do not look back at the previous list. Keep track of the number of times you are successful.

rabbit	stove
book	bear
mountain	pencil
rock	tent
telephone	key
robin	clock
cloud	tree
snow	fox

Most people find that many of the words presented above do not function as effective retrieval cues. Given the cue robin, for example, it is often difficult to remember the other member of the pair (flute). People who *do* find that the retrieval cues are effective are usually those who did not follow instructions. Note that the instructions were to simply read each word and to do nothing more. If you found that most of the cues presented above were effective, chances are that you used strategies similar to those discussed below.[8]

The demonstration experiment presented below is designed to illustrate strategies for making potential retrieval cues more effective. As in the preceding experiment, you will see sixteen pairs of words. This time, however, do not simply read each word as you proceed through the list. Instead, try to do something to relate both members of each pair. An excellent strategy for accomplishing this goal is to use imagery. For example, assume that you see the pair "chicken-flag." Imagine a chicken that is doing something with a flag, for example, holding it in its mouth. Try this strategy on each of the pairs presented below.

newspaper arrow	fork ball
bathtub whale	rain tuba
deer roller skates	apple magazine
rope football	cup yardstick
cake lawn mower	cigar piano
worm house	taxicab flower
fan gun	hat lion
shark peach	bus spear

The list below contains the first word from each member of the pairs presented above. Keep track of the number of times these words enable you to remember the second member of each pair. Most people find their performance on this list is much better than their performance on the earlier list (unless, of course, they "cheated" earlier and used a strategy that integrated each pair of words).[9]

rain	worm
cigar	fan
cake	fork
shark	apple
deer	hat
newspaper	rope
bathtub	bus
cup	taxicab

Remembering Faces and Names

We noted earlier that a problem faced by many people involves their inability to remember names of new acquaintances. A possible solution to this problem is to use a strategy known as the image-name technique, a strategy similar to the imagery strategy discussed above.[10]

The image-name technique is designed to establish a link between the unique facial features of an individual and the unique features of his or her name. To use this strategy, you first need to examine a person's facial features or qualities. Try to identify features that will enable you to differentiate the person's face from other, similar faces. For example, try to identify the unique features of the face in Figure 3.1 and use an acronym or acrostic to help you remember the unique features. When you are finished, turn the page and see if you can correctly select the identical face from the set of alternatives that occur in Figure 3.3.

The preceding strategy should help you differentiate similar-looking faces from one another (this can be important if you witness a crime, for example), but it will not necessarily help you remember the names that go with each face. To remember names, you should try to identify unique facial features that share a relationship with the person's name or with syllables of the name. The picture in Figure 3.2 provides an illustration of how this correspondence can be developed.

If you practice the image-name strategy (examples of faces and names are provided at the end of this chapter) you should become able to learn names quite effectively. This general strategy can also be used for other purposes. For example, waiters and waitresses may use it to remember what each customer ordered, and salespersons may use it to remember the family background and interests of clients they serve.

Using Familiar Structures as Retrieval Cues

Such strategies as linking two words by imagery or linking faces and names can result in excellent memory *given* that appropriate retrieval cues (one word from a pair or a person's face) are available (Figure 3.3). If appropriate cues are not provided, however, we often fail to retrieve information that is stored (for example, we may fail to retrieve the names of all people we know unless we see pictures of them). In addition, the pair-linking strategies do not preserve information about the order in which pairs occurred.

Figure 3.1
Try to remember this face.

The ancient Greeks invented some excellent strategies for solving many types of memory problems.[11] One strategy is called the *method of loci* (the method of using familiar locations). To use this strategy you must have a familiar sequence of visual images that can be recalled easily and used as retrieval cues. One example of a sequence of images would be scenes you can remember while imagining a familiar route, such as a route through your house (through the front door, to various places in the living room, and into the kitchen).

Here's how to use the scene you have imagined. Basically, you need to (1) form an image of each object to be remembered, and (2) "place" it in your imagined scene. Thus, if the first object is "horse," you might imagine it jumping through the front door of your house. If the second object is "rocket," you might imagine a huge rocket in the second location you come to in your house (on the couch). Ideally, the visual scene you use should have as many places or locations as there are objects to remember, and you should proceed through your scene in a natural order that is easy to remember. In addition, it can be helpful to form images that have vivid and unique interactions.

Below is a list of ten words to attempt to remember by using the method of loci. Spend enough time on each word to form an image of it and its place in your scene that is vivid and unique.

carrot	trumpet
moose	pillow
helicopter	scissors
Indian	goat
chicken	cherry

Without looking back at the list, try to recall the words in the order in which they occurred by using the retrieval cues in your familiar path. Now try to recall

Figure 3.2
Remembering names and faces. Distinctive facial features might include the beard and the glasses. Distinctive relationships between the facial features and the name (Bart Stein) might include letting "beard" remind you of a bar (for Bart) and "glasses" remind you of beer glasses, called steins (for Stein).

them *in reverse order*. This can be done quite easily by simply reversing the direction in which you move through your imaginary scene.

Consider the following memory problem. As quickly as possible, recall the fifth word from the preceding list, now the third, now the seventh, and so forth. Although it is possible to use the method of loci to achieve this goal, it can be very cumbersome and time consuming to walk through all the scenes while counting each one. A much better strategy for solving this type of memory problem is to use images indexed to a numerical code. The peg word system illustrates one such strategy. In the peg word system we form interactive images using objects that are associated by rhyme to numbers. For example, try forming interactive images using the objects in the peg word scheme below and the concepts in the previous word list (image a carrot in a bun or a moose with a shoe on its antlers).

One is a bun	Six is a stick
Two is a shoe	Seven is heaven
Three is a tree	Eight is a gate
Four is a door	Nine is a dime
Five is a hive	Ten is a hen

Figure 3.3
Try to identify the face that you saw earlier.

After using the peg word system you should be able to recall any numbered item in a word list by using the number as a cue to retrieve the word and images that were paired with it. Of course, to use this strategy effectively it is necessary to first become familiar with the peg word scheme so that the images can be retrieved with ease.

INVENTING YOUR OWN MEMORY TECHNIQUES

One of the most important and challenging ways to improve your memory is to become an inventor—an inventor of new memory techniques. For example, you might invent appropriate acronyms and acrostics (see our previous discussion of these devices). Additional techniques, such as the use of special rhymes and rules, might be invented as well. Assume you want to remember whether the head of a school is spelled "principle" or "principal." You might create a memory aid, such as, "The head of the school should be a *pal*."

Listed below are examples of memory problems many people encounter. Try to invent a technique for solving these problems. Possible answers (your answers might well be better) are provided in Appendix C.

In accounting, people must learn that the left column is used for entering debits and the right column is used for entering credits. Devise a scheme for remembering which is which.

People who spend a lot of time in the woods (hikers, campers, or hunters) need to know which kinds of snakes are poisonous and which are not. In general, snakes that have adjacent red and black stripes have no poison whereas those that have adjacent red and yellow stripes do. Devise a memory scheme that will help people remember which type of snake is which.

In boating, the term "port" is used for left and "starboard" for right. Devise a way to remember these facts.

Note that, for each of the problems presented above, the amount of information that needs to be remembered is rather small. The most difficult aspect of each problem is that it is easy to forget by confusing one thing with another, for example, by confusing poisonous snakes with nonpoisonous snakes or confusing "port" with "right" rather than "left." The ability to reduce forgetting and confusion therefore constitutes an important criterion for evaluating the efficacy of any memory techniques you invent.

A powerful strategy for enhancing memory is to store information externally (on paper) rather than attempt to remember it directly. This seems like an obvious strategy, but even here there is a considerable amount of room for human invention. Different ways of organizing information affect the ease of performing various tasks.

Imagine that you write a grocery list containing fifteen items, such as milk, cereal, apples, and dog food. Once you get to the grocery store there are several ways you might use this list. One is to get the first item on your list (milk), then the second (cereal), and so forth. If your items are not organized according to the sections in your grocery store, you will be forced to make a number of trips back and forth through the store.

Another way to use the grocery list is to walk to one section of the store (the dairy section) and scan your list for all items that may be found there (milk, eggs, and cheese). Next, walk to another section of the store (pet foods) and scan all the items again. This is more efficient than walking back and forth across the store, but it is still not optimal unless your list is organized in a way that fits the organization of your grocery store.

The problem of storing information in a way that enables us to obtain access to relevant information easily becomes especially important when the amount of information to be stored is large. Consider the information in the phone book for a relatively large city. This information is organized in a way that makes it relatively easy to find a phone number or street address if you know the name of a person. It is also easy to determine the number of people in a particular city who have the same last name. However, imagine that you want to know the phone numbers of all people who live on 21st Avenue, or who live in the eastern part of a city. You would have to search through every entry in the phone book to find this type of information. Needless to say, this would be a tedious procedure.

There are many situations in which externally stored information (frequently called a "data base") needs to be searched from a variety of perspectives. If you run a business, for example, you may want to call or send announcements to all people in your area of a city. Or you may sometimes want to send mailings only to those families whose income is over a certain amount per year, to those who have visited your store during the past year, and so forth. Similarly, if you make notes about articles and books that you have read you may sometimes like to see only those that were (1) written by certain authors; (2) written about particular topics; (3) humorous rather than nonhumorous; or (4) based on scientific research rather than personal experience. As our example with the phone book indicates, it can be very difficult to store information in ways that permits easy access to such categories.

Fortunately, modern computer technology is making it possible to gain access to data bases according to a variety of categories. For example, most microcomputers available for home use have programs that allow you access to such categories of information as authors and topics. The use of computers therefore provides a powerful strategy for enhancing memory. Nevertheless, computers depend on humans, so you must choose the format for representing and retrieving information that is most appropriate for your needs and purposes. Since the computer's ability to find various categories of information will depend on what you put into it, your ingenuity will have important effects on what the computer can do.

SUMMARY

Our discussion in this chapter emphasized the relationship between remembering and problem solving. We argued that people who are good at remembering information have developed effective problem-solving skills. First, they are able to *identify* and *define* situations that may cause memory difficulties ("this is too much information to hold in short-term memory" or "if I am not careful I will get confused and forget whether 'port' means right or left"). Second, they *explore* a variety of strategies and realize the need to select those appropriate for a particular memory task. Third, they *actively* try strategies and *look* at the effects on performance (that is, on their ability to remember). If their performance is poor, they reenter the IDEAL cycle and perhaps redefine the nature of the problem or select or invent different strategies. They then act on these changes and look at the effects, and hence continue to improve their memory skills.

Discussion in this chapter included information important for understanding the relationship between strategy selection and problem definition. First, we emphasized how particular strategies (simple rehearsal or categorization, for example) are appropriate for some memory tasks but not others. Second, we noted that storage of information does not guarantee its retrieval, and that the selection and evaluation of strategies must take the nature of the retrieval environment into account (if no retrieval cues are going to be provided, you need to generate a retrieval scheme of your own). Third, we discussed ways to increase the probability that particular retrieval cues will be effective (by forming interactive images, for example). Finally, we noted that the improvement of memory skills is an ongoing process. A major challenge is to become skilled at inventing new memory techniques for solving problems you may confront in everyday life.

EXERCISES

1. Carefully read the passage below once, and then turn to the answer section in the back of this book and answer the questions about it.

   You are the driver of a bus that can hold a total of 72 passengers (there are 36 seats that can each hold 2 passengers). At the first stop 7 people get on the bus. At the next stop 3 people get off and 5 get on. At the next stop 4 people get off and 2 get on. During each of the next two stops, 3 passengers get off and 2 get on. At the next stop 5 passengers get off and 7 get on the bus. When the bus arrives at the next to the last stop, 2 people get on and 5 get off.

   Develop acronyms or other techniques for remembering the following.

2. The order of the cranial nerves is olfactory, optic, oculomotor, trochlear, trigeminal, abducens, facial, auditory, glossopharyngeal, vagus, spinal-accessory, and hypoglossal.
3. You should set the clock 1 hour ahead in the spring and an hour back in the fall (for daylight savings time).

Devise strategies for remembering the following.

4. The combination to your new lock is 22-4-9.

5. Balsam fir trees have smooth twigs; Eastern hemlocks have rough twigs.

Devise a strategy to help you remember the correct spelling for each word below.

Correct spelling	*Common misspelling*
6. across	accross
7. facilitate	facillitate
8. development	developement

Devise a technique for remembering the facts associated with each name when you are presented with the name

9.	Edmund Hillary	First to climb Mount Everest
10.	Hubert Booth	Invented the vacuum cleaner
11.	Frank T. Cary	Chairman of IBM

Devise a strategy to remember the names associated with each face below.

12. Harriet Eisely

13. Lynn Foreman

14. Rose Lipman

NOTES

[1]F. Bacon, *Novum organum*. First book, Aphorism 2, 1620.

[2]Studies of the effectiveness of various types of memory strategies include: G. H. Bower and M. C. Clark, Narrative stories as mediators for serial learning, *Psychonomic Science, 14,* 181–182; 1969; F. I. M. Craik and R. S. Lockhart, Levels of processing: A framework for memory research, *Journal of Verbal Learning and Verbal Behavior, 11,* 671–684; 1972; F. I. M. Craik and M. J. Watkins, The role of rehearsal in short-term memory, *Journal of Verbal Learning and Verbal Behavior, 12,* 599–607, 1973; T. S. Hyde and J. J. Jenkins, Differential effects of incidental tasks on the organization of recall of a list of highly associated words, *Journal of Experimental Psychology, 82,* 472–481, 1969; D. Rundus and R. C. Atkinson, Rehearsal processes in free recall: A procedure for direct observation, *Journal of Verbal Learning and Verbal Behavior, 9,* 99–105, 1970; K. A. Wollen, A. Weber, and D. H. Lowry, Bizarreness versus interaction of mental images as determinants of learning, *Cognitive Psychology, 2,* 518–523, 1972.

[3]T. J. Keeney, S. R. Cannizzo, and J. H. Flavell, Spontaneous and induced verbal rehearsal in a recall task, *Child Development, 38,* 953–966, 1967.

[4]G. A. Miller, The magical number seven plus or minus two: Some limits on our capacity for processing information, *Psychological Review, 63,* 81–97, 1956.

[5]Studies illustrating how particular strategies may or may not be effective depending on the testing context include: C. D. Morris, J. D. Bransford, and J. J. Franks, Levels of processing versus transfer appropriate processing, *Journal of Verbal Learning and Verbal Behavior, 16,* 519–533, 1977; B. S. Stein, Depth of processing re-examined: The effects of precision of encoding and test appropriateness, *Journal of Verbal Learning and Verbal Behavior, 17,* 165–174, 1978.

[6]E. Tulving, Cue-dependent forgetting, *American Scientist, 62,* 74–82, 1974.

[7]E. Tulving, Relation between encoding specificity and levels of processing. In L. S. Cermak and F. I. M. Craik (Eds.), *Levels of Processing and Human Memory.* Hillsdale; N.J.: Erlbaum, 1978.

[8]B. S. Stein, The effects of cue-target uniqueness on cued recall performance. *Memory and Cognition, 5,* 319–322, 1977.

[9]K. A. Wollen, A. Weber, and D. H. Lowry, Bizarreness versus interaction of mental images as determinants of learning. *Cognitive Psychology, 2,* 518–523, 1972.

[10]Strategies for linking faces and names are discussed in: K. L. Higbee, *Your Memory: How It Works and How to Improve It*. Englewood Cliffs, N.J.: Prentice-Hall, 1977; H. Lorayne and J. Lucas, *The Memory Book*. New York: Ballantine, 1974.

[11]F. Yates, *The Art of Memory*. London: Routledge & Kegan Paul, 1966.

SUGGESTED READINGS

Practically Oriented Readings

Bellezza, F. S., *Improve Your Memory Skills*. Englewood Cliffs, N.J.: Prentice-Hall, 1982.

Bower, G. H., Analysis of a mnemonic device, *American Scientist, 58,* 496–510, 1970.

Cermak, L. S., *Improving Your Memory*. New York: McGraw-Hill, 1976.

Higbee, K. L., *Your Memory: How It Works and How to Improve It*. Englewood Cliffs, N.J.: Prentice-Hall, 1977.

Lorayne, H., and J. Lucas, *The Memory Book*. New York: Ballantine, 1974.

Luria, A. R., *The Mind of a Mnemonist*. New York: Basic Books, 1968.

Theoretically Oriented Readings

Ellis, H. C., and R. R. Hunt, *Fundamentals of Human Memory and Cognition* (3rd Ed.). Dubuque, Iowa: W. C. Brown, 1983.

Klatzky, R. L., *Human Memory: Structure and Process* (2nd Ed.). San Francisco: W. H. Freeman, 1980.

Neisser, U., *Memory Observed: Remembering in Natural Contexts*. San Francisco: W. H. Freeman, 1982.

Zechmeister, E. G., and S. E. Nyberg, *Human Memory: An Introduction to Research and Theory*. Monterey, Calif.: Brooks/Cole, 1982.

4

LEARNING WITH UNDERSTANDING

Dear Jill,

Remember Sally, the person I mentioned in my last letter? You'll never guess what she did this week. First, she let loose a team of gophers. The plan backfired when a dog chased them away. She then threw a party but the guests failed to bring their motorcycles. Furthermore, her stereo system was not loud enough. Sally spent the next day looking for a "Peeping Tom" but was unable to find one in the yellow pages. Obscene phone calls gave her some hope until the number was changed. It was the installation of blinking neon lights across the street that finally did the trick. Sally framed the ad from the classified section and now has it hanging on her wall.

Love,
Bill[1]

Discussion in Chapter 3 emphasized strategies for remembering information. Memory strategies are very helpful, of course, but it is important to note that all the memory problems in the previous chapter involved information that was already comprehensible to you. A major goal of this chapter is to show that the problem of comprehending new information—of learning with understanding—is different from the problem of merely memorizing that information. *The strategies necessary to solve comprehension problems therefore differ from those necessary for memorization.*

We begin by showing how comprehension involves problem solving. Consider the letter about Sally at the top of this page. Please read it (even if you have already done so) and try to notice the mental processes that you utilize in order to comprehend. Please begin now.

COMPREHENSION AS PROBLEM SOLVING

Most people have difficulty understanding the letter about Sally. They understand each word. The problem is not one of too many technical terms. Nevertheless, something seems to be missing. In short, most people *identify* the existence of a problem; namely, that they do not fully comprehend.

Most readers also try to *define* the nature of their problem. One possibility is that the letter is gibberish. Another is that the passage presupposes some information not available to them (but which may be available to the recipient of the letter). Most people then *explore* various strategies for solution. For example, they may generate possible reasons for Sally's activities (maybe she's in love with somebody), *actively* attempt to use their hypothesis to understand the passage, and *look* at the effects. If their initial hypothesis doesn't work they may generate alternate hypotheses and test them. Hence they may move through the IDEAL cycle a number of times.

Most people have difficulty solving the Sally problem. If you are in this situation, it is instructive to notice what effects this can have. One is that it is relatively difficult to remember what Sally did. Another is that you are unable to answer a host of inference questions. For example,

1. Where did Sally put the gophers?
2. Why did Sally want the guests to bring motorcycles?
3. Whose number was changed?
4. Who probably made the calls?
5. What did the advertisement say?

If you fail to understand the letter about Sally, it is extremely difficult to answer such questions.

The letter becomes much more comprehensible when one is supplied with appropriate information. This information functions as a powerful conceptual tool that allows people to remember more effectively as well as to answer inference questions. The information required to understand the passage about Sally involves information about her goal, namely, that she is trying to get a neighbor to move. Given this information, it is instructive to read the passage again and to then try to answer inference questions such as those noted above.

Comprehension and Inferences

The passage about Sally was written especially to illustrate how comprehension depends on the activation of additional knowledge. Similar processes seem to be involved in all instances of comprehension; people are often surprised when helped to notice the degree to which they spontaneously utilize previously acquired knowledge in order to comprehend. Consider the following passage.[2]

A thirsty ant went to a river. He became carried away by the rush of the stream and was about to drown. A dove was sitting in a tree overhanging the water. The dove plucked a leaf and let it fall. The leaf fell into the stream close to the ant and the ant climbed onto it. The ant floated safely to the bank. Shortly afterward, a birdcatcher came and laid a trap in the tree. The ant saw his plan and stung him on the foot. In pain the birdcatcher threw down his trap. The noise made the bird fly away.

A number of assumptions are necessary to understand this story. For example, readers usually assume that the ant walked to the river and the dove flew to the tree, although this information was never explicitly presented. Similarly, readers realize that an ant might drown because it requires oxygen (it would be strange to worry about a fish drowning in a river), that the dove probably plucked the leaf with its beak, and so forth. Basic information about doves and ants therefore plays an important role in guiding the inferences readers make.

Additional sets of inferences must also be made to understand the ant and dove story. One important set of inferences involves assumptions about the characters' goals. For example, most people assume that the dove plucked the leaf to save the ant, that the bird catcher's plan was to trap the dove, and that the ant bit the bird catcher to repay the dove for its previous favor. Note that none of this information is stated in the story; in each case it is generated by the reader. Indeed, the story does not even state that the ant and the dove saw each other. The author of the passage did not need to explicitly present this information; it was assumed that readers would supply it. Communication would be extremely cumbersome if speakers and writers had to explicitly provide all the information necessary for comprehension. If people lack relevant background knowledge, however, they are unable to make the assumptions necessary to understand in ways that speakers and writers intend.[3]

Read the following statements, and see if you can determine what background information you need to make the statements comprehensible (see Appendix D for possible answers).

1. The man was late for work because it snowed.
2. I drove my wife to work because her bicycle had a flat tire.
3. The policeman held up his hand and the cars stopped.[4]

The Role of Conceptual Knowledge

Here is another comprehension problem that, in many ways, is analogous to the Sally passage.

Dear Jim,

Remember Pete, the guy I described in my last letter? You'll never guess what he did last week. First, he talked about the importance of mass spectrometers. He then discussed the isotopes of argon 36 and argon 38 and noted that they were of higher density than expected. He also cited the high values of neon found in the atmosphere. He has a paper that is already written, but he is aware of the need for further investigation as well.

Love,
Sandra

Like the letter about Sally, this letter should be difficult to comprehend. One reason for the difficulty is that you do not know Pete's goal. His goal is to argue that data gathered from a NASA spaceship's voyage to Venus calls into question current theories about the formation of our solar system.

It is instructive to ask whether information about Pete's goal is sufficient to allow you to comprehend the letter. Most people feel that it helps comprehension to some extent. However, unless they are knowledgeable about astronomy, they are unable to make many inferences about the letter. For example:

1. To what extent do high levels of the isotopes of argon have anything to do with theories of the formation of the solar system?
2. Why are high values of neon significant for this question, or are they?
3. How do these questions relate to the importance of mass spectrometers?

Information about Pete's goals does not suddenly permit answers to such inference questions.

It seems clear that the only way to solve the problem of comprehending the letter about Pete is to learn about concepts that underlie the science of astronomy. Without knowledge of relevant core concepts, it is impossible to solve a variety of problems solvable by experts in this field. As noted in Chapter 2, knowledge of core concepts in a field *simplifies* problem solving. Nevertheless, it is not necessarily simple to acquire these concepts in the first place. The problem of learning about new areas of knowledge is discussed next.

LEARNING ABOUT NEW AREAS OF KNOWLEDGE

One of the best ways to gain information about processes of learning is to consider the problem of acquiring expertise in various areas, such as mathematics, physics, biology, and psychology. For example, assume that you know only a little about biology and that your goal is to develop more expertise in this area. Assume further that the current lesson involves veins and arteries. You might therefore read a text stating that arteries are thick and elastic and carry blood rich in oxygen from the heart. Veins are thinner and less elastic and carry blood rich in carbon dioxide back to the heart. For novices, even this relatively simple set of facts can seem arbitrary and confusing. Was it veins or arteries that are thin? Was the thin one or the thick one elastic? Which one carries carbon dioxide from the heart (or was it to the heart)?

The problem of arbitrariness faced by novices can be mimicked by using simple sentences that are highly comprehensible to nearly everyone. The demonstration presented below, which involves statements about a group of people, provides an illustration.[5] Spend no more than a few seconds reading each of the sentences presented below.

The fat one bought the padlock.
The strong one cleaned the paintbrush.
The cheerful one read the newspaper.
The skinny one purchased the scissors.

The funny one admired the ring.
The toothless one plugged in the cord.
The barefoot one climbed the steps.
The bald one cut out the coupon.
The sleepy one held the pitcher.
The blind one closed the bag.
The kind one opened the milk.
The poor one entered the museum.

Now try to answer the following questions without looking back at the preceding sentences.

Which one purchased the scissors?
Which one cut out the coupon?
Which one climbed the steps?
Which one closed the bag?
Which one read the newspaper?
Which one cleaned the paintbrush?
Which one admired the ring?
Which one held the pitcher?
Which one plugged in the cord?
Which one bought the padlock?
Which one entered the museum?
Which one opened the milk?

Most people have a difficult time remembering which type of person performed a particular activity. The major reason for this difficulty is that the relationship between each type and the actions performed seem arbitrary: there is no clear reason a particular type of person should perform a particular type of activity. Novices in the field of biology are in a similar position when trying to learn about such structures as veins and arteries; relationships between these entities and their properties seem arbitrary. For example, novices are unable to see why arteries should be elastic or nonelastic, thick or thin.

There are several ways to approach the problem of learning information that initially seems arbitrary. One is simply to rehearse the facts until they are mastered ("artery, thick, elastic"; "artery, thick, elastic"). A more efficient approach is to use memory techniques similar to those discussed in Chapter 3.[6] The use of imagery techniques provides one illustration. That arteries are thick could be remembered by forming an image of a thick, hollow tube that flashes "artery." That arteries are elastic could be remembered by imagining that the tube is suspended by a rubber band that stretches and contracts, thereby causing the tube to move up and down. You could also embellish the image by having red liquid (blood) and round (like an *o*) bubbles (oxygen) pouring out of the tube, and these could be moving in a direction away from an image of a Valentine's Day heart. This composite image could serve as a basis for remembering that arteries are thick and elastic and carry blood rich in oxygen away from the heart. An alternate technique is to use verbal elaborations; for example, "*Art*(ery) was *thick* around the middle so he wore pants with an elastic waistband."

Memory Strategies versus Comprehension Strategies

Examples like the one just discussed show how such strategies as the use of imagery can be used to improve the retention of facts. Similar strategies were discussed in Chapter 3. Since people who are attempting to learn about new areas (for example, about veins and arteries) face the problem of trying to remember facts and relationships that initially seem arbitrary, these techniques appear to be a powerful way to learn.

It is important to note, however, that, from the present perspective at least, the ultimate goal of learning is to acquire information that can be used as conceptual tools to facilitate subsequent problem solving. People who simply memorize new facts are frequently unable to use this information to solve new problems. Imagine that people remember "arteries are elastic" either by imagining a rubber band holding a tube or "thick-waisted Art(ery) and his elastic waistband." What if these people are confronted with the problem of designing an artificial artery? Would it have to be elastic? What are the potential implications of hardening of the arteries? Would this have a serious impact on people's health? Learners who used the previously mentioned techniques to remember that arteries are elastic would have little basis for answering these questions. Indeed, the "rubber band" and "waistband" techniques could easily lead to misinterpretation: Perhaps hardening of the arteries affects people's abilities to stretch their arms and legs.

Memory techniques are useful for many purposes, but one must take a very different approach to learning to develop an understanding of veins and arteries. Effective learners attend to factual content, but they also try to understand the significance or relevance of facts. For example, the passage about veins and arteries stated that arteries are elastic. What is the significance of elasticity? How does this property relate to the functions arteries perform? An effective learner may seek information that can clarify this relationship. For example, our imaginary passage states that arteries carry blood from the heart, blood that is pumped in spurts. This provides one clue about the significance of elasticity—arteries may need to expand and contract to accommodate the pumping of blood. Some learners might then ask why veins do *not* need to be elastic. Because veins carry blood back to the heart, perhaps they have less need to accommodate the large changes in pressure resulting from the heart pumping blood in spurts.

Some learners may carry this process a step further. Because arteries carry blood *from* the heart, there is a problem of directionality. Why does the blood not flow back into the heart? This will not be identified as a problem if one assumes that arterial blood always flows downhill, but suppose our passage mentions that there are arteries in the neck and shoulder regions. Arterial blood must therefore flow uphill as well. This information might provide an additional clue about the significance of elasticity. If arteries expand from a spurt of blood and then contract, this might help the blood move in a particular direction. The elasticity of arteries might therefore serve the function of a one-way valve that enables blood to flow forward but not back. If one were to design an artificial artery, it might therefore be possible to equip it with valves and hence make it nonelastic. However, this solution might work only if the spurts of blood did not cause too much pressure on the artificial artery.

Our imaginary passage does not provide enough information about pressure requirements, so a learner would have to look elsewhere for this information. Note, however, that our learner realizes the need to obtain additional information. The learner's activities are not unlike those employed by good detectives or researchers when they confront a new problem. Although their initial assumptions about the significance of various facts may ultimately be found to be incorrect, the act of seeking clarification is fundamental to the development of new expertise. In contrast, the person who simply concentrates on techniques for memorizing facts does not know whether there is something more to be understood.

Arbitrary Sentences Reconsidered

The importance of searching for information that can clarify the significance or relevance of facts and relationships can also be illustrated by reconsidering the set of sentences about different types of people. We noted earlier that memory strategies can be used to help us retain important information. Nevertheless, these techniques do not help people understand *why* each type might perform a particular activity.

An alternate way to approach the problem of learning about the different types is to try to figure out why each might be appropriate for a particular activity. This is analogous to asking why certain entities (veins or arteries) have the particular structures and functions they do. The following list of sentences is identical to that presented earlier, except that each sentence contains an elaboration that should help you understand why it might be appropriate for each person to perform a particular activity. Read the sentences through once, and then attempt to answer the questions presented below:

The fat one bought the padlock to place on the refrigerator door.
The strong one cleaned the paintbrush used to paint the barbells.
The cheerful one read the newspaper announcing that he had won the lottery.
The skinny one purchased the scissors to use when taking in her pants.
The funny one admired the ring that squirted water.
The toothless one plugged in the cord to the food blender.
The barefoot one climbed the steps leading to the vat of grapes.
The bald one cut out the coupon for the hair tonic.
The sleepy one held the pitcher containing water for the coffee machine.
The blind one closed the bag after feeding her seeing-eye dog.
The kind one opened the milk to give to the hungry child.
The poor one entered the museum to get shelter from the snowstorm.

Here are some questions about the preceding sets of sentences:

Which one purchased the scissors?
Which one cut out the coupon?
Which one climbed the steps?
Which one closed the bag?
Which one read the newspaper?
Which one cleaned the paintbrush?
Which one admired the ring?
Which one held the pitcher?
Which one plugged in the cord?
Which one bought the padlock?
Which one entered the museum?
Which one opened the milk?

Most people find it relatively easy to remember who did what when they receive elaborations clarifying reasons for certain activities. These elaborations must be precise, however; that is, they must help one understand why each type would perform a particular activity. Other kinds of elaborations can make sense semantically and yet be imprecise: These can actually hurt memory performance rather than help. Examples of imprecise elaborations for the set of sentences presented above are as follows.

The fat one bought the padlock to place on the garage door.
The strong one cleaned the paintbrush used to paint the chair.
The cheerful one read the newspaper bought at the newstand.
The skinny one purchased the scissors to use when trimming her nails.
The funny one admired the ring in the jewelry store.

Similarly, a statement such as "arteries are elastic so that they can carry blood" is relatively imprecise.

Further Illustrations of Memory versus Comprehension Strategies

It is useful to consider additional illustrations of strategies that can be used to memorize facts and relationships versus those necessary to understand the significance or relevance of these relationships. Consider first the pairs of scissors shown in Figure 4.1.[7] Imagine that you study until you can draw each pair of scissors from memory. This provides no guarantee that you understand how the physical features of each pair of scissors are related to its unique function. Table 4.1 lists the primary function of each pair of scissors illustrated above. Given this information, the particular structure of each pair is more meaningful. It becomes clear that relationships between each scissor's structure and function are not arbitrary; for example, the structure of the dressmaker's shears allows people to cut on a flat surface. The ability to understand the significance or relevance of features has a number of potential benefits. One is that people who understand these relationships should be in a good position to invent a new pair of scissors that allows them to perform particular tasks more efficiently. They certainly should be better equipped to create useful inventions than would people who merely memorized differences in appearances without understanding the functions each served.

As another example of differences between memorization and comprehension strategies, imagine reading a text that contains these statements: "The Indians of the Northwest Coast lived in slant-roofed houses built of cedar plank. . . . Some California Indian tribes lived in simple earth-covered or brush shelters. . . . The Plains Indians lived mainly in teepees. . . ."[8] You could undoubtedly create some type of memory aid that enabled you to remember which American Indian tribe had which type of house. Nevertheless, this is a far cry from understanding the significance of the information. To achieve the latter, you would need to understand why different tribes chose different types of houses. For example, you would need to consider how the style of house related to the geographic area in which the American Indians lived (house style would undoubtedly be affected by type of climate as well as by the raw materials available for building). The style of house would also undoubtedly be related to life-style. For example, teepees are relatively portable, whereas cedar plank houses are not.

It is instructive to note that the preceding example was taken from a story written for elementary school children. The information presented to the children seemed arbitrary; no attempt was made to supply elaborations explaining why different tribes chose the houses they did. This problem of the apparent arbitrariness of texts occurs at all age levels, from elementary school to college.[9] One reason is that writers of such texts are usually experts in their particular domains whereas the readers are often novices. To the writers, the texts do not seem arbitrary because they (the writers) can implicitly "fill in the gaps." For example, they already know why arteries are elastic or why various American Indians choose certain styles of houses; in short, they not only know the facts, they also

Figure 4.1
Some examples of different types of scissors.

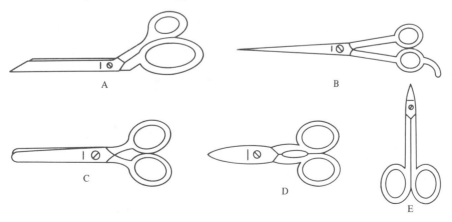

Table 4.1
Some Functions for the Scissors Illustrated in Figure 4.1

Structure	Function
a. Dressmaker's shears	
Heavy	Because of heavy use
One hole larger than other	Two or three fingers will fit in larger hole—allows greater steadiness as one cuts cloth on flat surface
Blades off-center and aligned with finger-hole edge	Blade can rest on table surface as cloth is cut—again, greater steadiness
b. Barber's shears	
Very sharp	To cut thin material, for example, hair
Pointed	Permits blades to snip close to scalp and to snip very small strands of hair
Hook on finger hole	A rest for one finger, which allows scissors to be supported when held at various angles—hence, greater maneuverability
c. Pocket or children's scissors	
Blunt ends	Scissors can be carried in pocket without cutting through cloth; children can handle without poking themselves or others
Short blades	Allow greater control by the gross motor movements of the child just learning to cut
d. Nail scissors	
Wide and thick at pivot point	To withstand pressure from cutting thick and rigid materials, that is, nails
Slightly curved blades	To cut slightly curved nails
e. Cuticle scissors	
Very sharp blade	To cut semielastic materials, for example, skin of cuticles
Small, curved blades	To allow maneuverability necessary to cut small curved area
Long extension from finger holes to joint	As compensation for short blades, necessary for holding.

already understand the significance of these facts. To the novice, however, the extra knowledge necessary to fill in the gaps is not available. Novices are therefore often forced to resort to the technique of memorizing information without really understanding it.

It is hoped that, as you become better able to spot arbitrariness in texts, you will also become more likely to search in other sources or to ask questions that can help you *understand* what you learn rather than merely memorize. It is important to note, however, that the processes necessary to achieve understanding are frequently more complex than those necessary for merely memorizing information. It is therefore helpful to think again about the ultimate goal of learning: to develop conceptual tools that make it easier to solve a variety of important problems. The mere memorization of information rarely provides tools that enable one to solve new problems later on.

Note Taking

As discussed in the preceding sections, the search for information that clarifies the significance of facts can take a considerable amount of time. It can therefore be important to preserve the material we are trying to master until we are able to explore relationships more carefully. Such activities require effective note-taking skills.

A lack of note-taking skills can hinder learning in a number of ways. One involves the failure to write down important types of information, perhaps because of the erroneous belief that, "I will surely remember this." Another frequent problem with notes is that people write down cues that are too vague. As a simple illustration, imagine that you write down "American Indian houses" yet include no additional information to remind you of the significance of this information. You may then have a difficult time remembering that this was the topic of a passage used to illustrate the problem of the arbitrariness of facts.

An obvious way to overcome the problem of vague cues is to record all the information that will be used. However, in many cases the exact wording of a message is not important or there is simply not enough time to write the complete message. In these situations it is necessary to use an abbreviated form of the message in our notes. When constructing such notes, most people focus on the main points or key concepts in a message and then incorporate these ideas into a list or outline. These types of notes may provide ineffective retrieval cues for reconstructing the underlying relationships. For example, try using the following outline to reconstruct the underlying joke.[10] (See Appendix D for a description of the joke.)

I. Theatre joke
  A. Good news
    1. Balcony
    2. Flames reach in several minutes
  B. Bad news
    1. Theatre fire
    2. Don't tell

One of the problems with this outline is that it does not help us understand the ordering of information in the joke or what the punch line is. The method used to represent the information is not appropriate for the task. Many other forms of notes can be used to help us understand and remember information. For example,

Figure 4.2
An illustration of lecture notes.

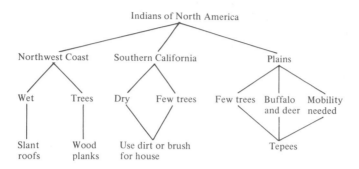

diagrams and graphs are typically considered visual aids, but they are often the most precise way to represent relationships among concepts. Figure 4.2 illustrates a treelike structure to represent the information presented in the paragraph about American Indian houses. In some cases it can also be valuable to include illustrations that help us understand the significance of facts (see Figure 4.3).

The particular form of notes that work best obviously depend on the nature of the materials to be learned and on how that information is to be used. Therefore, the selection of a note-taking strategy should involve the careful identification and definition of the underlying problem you need to solve.

Figure 4.3
Some diagrams that may help people understand the significance of facts.

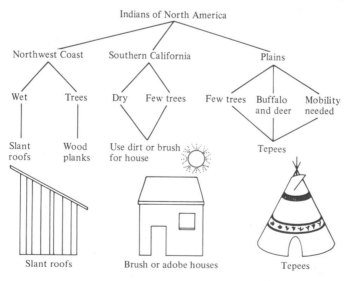

DEFINING THE LEVEL OF UNDERSTANDING

Previous discussion has emphasized that knowledge of concepts is necessary to solve a variety of problems (for example, to understand many statements about astronomy) and that, while learning about concepts, we must use strategies that allow us to comprehend the significance of new information rather than merely memorize it. However, how do we know whether we have learned enough about a topic and understand it adequately? For example, how do we know when we can stop studying for a test or stop the background reading for a talk? There is no simple answer to this question. Concepts can be learned at different *levels of precision,* and the level of precision necessary depends on the nature of the problems you eventually need to solve.

As an illustration of different levels of precision, assume that a group of people read a passage about veins and arteries, such as the one described earlier. Some people may feel that they have learned enough about this topic when they know that veins and arteries are parts of the body as opposed to, say, parts of a car engine. Other people may not feel that they have learned enough until they know that veins and arteries carry blood rather than serve some other bodily function, such as connect muscle to bone. Still other people may study until they know how veins and arteries are similar and different in terms of structure and function. For example, they may feel it is important to know that arteries are more elastic than veins and to understand why.

Note that the differences in the level of precision of people's knowledge may or may not be important for subsequent performance. Assume, for example, that they are asked a multiple-choice question.

Arteries are
a. good to eat
b. a type of insect
c. an important part of the body
d. sold only at gas stations
e. a kind of tree

One needs little information about arteries in order to answer such a question. In contrast, consider the following question.

Arteries   .
a. are more elastic than veins
b. carry blood that is pumped from the heart
c. are less elastic than veins
d. both a and b
e. both b and c

This question requires that the learner have a considerable amount of information about arteries. Even for this question, however, a person may be able to answer correctly yet still fail to understand *why* arteries are more elastic. This person might therefore fail to answer additional questions he or she was asked.

As an additional illustration of levels of precision, note that nearly all adults know the concept of "gold," as in "gold watch" or "valuable metal."[11] The level of precision of their understanding is sufficient to perform a variety of activities. For example, most of us can differentiate a gold ring from a silver ring and we know what is being referred to when people talk about the price of gold.

However, assume that you are presented with 100 large rocks. Of these, 99 are fool's gold and 1 is real gold. You may keep one rock. To solve this problem you need a technical concept of gold, the kind readily available to geologists but not to most other people. Our everyday concept of gold is precise enough for many types of activities, but it is not sufficiently precise to solve a problem such as the differentiation of real gold from fool's gold.

As another illustration of differences in levels of precision, imagine a young child who knows that airports are places where planes take off and land but who knows nothing more about them.[12] In contrast, adults know a great deal about airports, for example, that they are places where one can purchase tickets and that they contain metal detectors (and why).

Despite being limited, the child's knowledge of airports is sufficient for many purposes. For example, the child should be able to comprehend the statement, "We are going to the airport because Aunt Jane is coming to visit." However, assume that the child hears the statement, "Ruth decided not to wear her matching silver earrings, necklace, and belt because she wanted to avoid delays at the airport." Most adults who hear this statement assume that Ruth wants to avoid problems with metal detectors. Since the child doesn't have this knowledge, he or she has a difficult time understanding the statement about Ruth.

Evaluating Levels of Precision

Many people have difficulty determining if they have reached an appropriate level of precision because they have no clear criterion for evaluating their understanding other than the feedback they receive from other people (for example, tutors, professors, or supervisors). Although it is important to effectively use external sources of feedback, most successful learners also try to develop their own internal criteria for evaluating their learning. To develop such criteria, successful learners often try to devise tests that model or simulate the kinds of problems they expect to confront (designing artificial arteries or explaining the principles of astronomy). These tests give people the opportunity to actively apply their knowledge and, ideally, to discover any confusions, uncertainties, or gaps in their understanding. Such activities serve a function similar to the simulations and tests used by NASA to uncover possible problems that might be encountered by astronauts on space missions.

The importance of discovering gaps in our understanding can be illustrated by reading the paragraph below.

This is a two-player game. Each player is given a deck of cards numbered 0 through 9. The cards are placed face down in front of each player. Each player turns over the top card of his or her deck. If the sum of the two cards that are face up equals 10, they are removed from the table. If they do not equal 10 the player takes back the card and places it back in the deck and then shuffles it. The game stops when the winner has no cards left.

We have presented this game description to many students in our classes with instructions to either memorize the description or evaluate its usefulness in teaching addition to young children. We have also asked people who read this description to answer the following questions. Please do so now.

1. Would learning the rules improve your chances of winning?
2. If you played this game fifty times, how many games would you expect to win?
3. Estimate how long it would take to complete each game?

Despite the fact that most people believe they understand this game, their answers to the questions above suggest otherwise. The correct answers for these questions are no, 0, and forever, respectively. Most people fail to detect inconsistencies in the rules of the game that would make it impossible to win or end. This failure results in part from the failure to actively apply the rules to a real game situation. If you still have not found the inconsistencies in the rules, try working through an actual game mentally, or try using real cards (answers appear in Appendix D).

This example illustrates that an important part of evaluating our learning involves the active application of ideas to specific situations. If we know we are able to use a set of rules to play a game, solve a mathematical problem, or produce a concrete model, then we have acquired a better understanding of our own understanding. In the game description provided above, information that makes the game impossible to win or end was deliberately inserted. In other learning tasks the discovery of such inconsistencies is a clear signal that either our level of comprehension is not adequate or there is something deficient in the material we are trying to understand. In either case the detection of inconsistencies serves as a signal for *identifying* a problem and reentering the IDEAL cycle.

Problems of Access

The examples discussed above suggest that an important approach to the problem of evaluating your own learning is to consider the conditions under which information must be utilized. If you knew you would be asked to differentiate real gold from fool's gold, it would be clear that you needed more than your everyday knowledge of this concept. Similarly, when studying about veins and arteries it can be useful to imagine that you want to achieve understanding of the implications of hardening of the arteries. Such goals provide guidelines for determining the level of detail that is important to learn.

When thinking about the conditions under which knowledge must be used, it is also important to consider the degree to which the task environment provides cues that can help you access or retrieve appropriate knowledge. People frequently fail to solve problems *not* because they have failed to acquire relevant knowledge but because they fail to gain access to it when needed.

Here is a problem we have given to a number of college students who were enrolled in our courses on learning and memory.

> Professor X claims that students who have difficulty in school do so because they have a much higher forgetting rate than do more successful students. He supports his claim with the following study. A group of academically successful and less successful fifth graders read a story during school on Monday. The next day they are all asked to recall as much of the story as they can. On the average, the successful students recall 80 percent of the story correctly; the corresponding score for the less successful students is 65 percent. Professor X argues that these data support his claims about forgetting rates. Can you find problems with his argument?

Many students in our learning and memory classes have generated weak answers to this problem. Some say, "He studied only fifth graders; maybe it's not true for kids in other grades." Others state, "You can't prove much by only a single study." Although these statements have some validity, they nevertheless miss the most crucial flaw in Professor X's reasoning. He claims to have studied forgetting, yet he hasn't shown that the less successful students learned as much initially. Perhaps due to lack of attention or lack of previously acquired knowledge, the less successful students didn't learn as much about the story in the first place. Without some knowledge of initial learning (for example, give the children a test right after they hear the story), one cannot make claims about the rate at which forgetting occurred.

As we noted above, many college students fail to find the most crucial flaw in Professor X's argument. The interesting point is that this failure is not necessarily due to a lack of knowledge. We gave students this problem after they had studied forgetting; lectures had emphasized that the concept of forgetting presupposes someone has learned something in the first place (you cannot forget something you haven't learned). The students' failure therefore stemmed from a failure to *access* relevant information. Additional evidence for this point stems from the second part to our experiment. Approximately 5 minutes after the students had first attempted to solve the problem we gave it to them a second time. This time, however, we said, "Note our earlier discussions of relationships between forgetting and previous learning." Given this hint, the vast majority of the students noticed the flaw in Professor X's experimental design. Ideally, however, they should not have to rely on such hints.

Here is another example of overreliance on particular types of hints or clues.[13] A graduate student we know was studying for a test in statistics. The first test covered a number of chapters on probability theory; the course instructor had provided study sheets for each chapter. The graduate student found that he could easily solve each of the problem sets provided by the course instructor, so he was convinced he was ready for the test. At this point one of us took out a pair of scissors, cut out the test questions from each problem sheet, and mixed them up. Under these conditions the graduate student could not solve the problems. He had inadvertently been relying on knowledge of which chapter each problem came from to decide which formula to apply. When this information was no longer available he suddenly discovered a problem with the way he had initially learned the information. He therefore changed his study strategy and paid much more attention to questions about when and why particular formulas should be used.[14]

EVALUATING AND DEBUGGING OUR LEARNING STRATEGIES

No matter how carefully you try to anticipate the context in which information must be used (for example to anticipate the nature of a test or the questions that will be asked at a meeting), you will undoubtedly not always do this flawlessly. As a result, you will find yourself unable to answer questions. This can have negative consequences, such as a lower grade in a course and feelings of embarrassment at a meeting. The most important thing to do in such situations is to try to discover the reason for your error (define your problem) and resolve to avoid making the same mistake again. People who program computers use the word *debugging* to refer to situations in which they must figure out why a program they have written won't run (they have to "get the bugs out").[15] The idea of developing debugging strategies for all our activities is an important one to pursue.

Many people adopt strategies that make debugging difficult, if not impossible. After receiving a relatively poor score on a test, for example, many students avoid looking at the test in any detail: they try to forget about this unpleasantness. It is natural to want to avoid unpleasant situations. Nevertheless, this is also a surefire way to keep from learning from one's mistakes.

If you have difficulty with a topic despite having studied it, there are several debugging strategies that can help you define the nature of your problem more precisely. First, look at the types of questions you could answer versus those you could not answer. Did the ones you missed require more precision of understanding than you had acquired? You should also try to discover the sources of the information necessary to answer the questions that you missed. Were they in the text? In your notes? If they were, you were overlooking information, perhaps because you failed to realize that it could be important for understanding certain situations. If the relevant information was neither in your notes nor in the book, chances are that you need to work on effective note-taking skills.

Professors and other experts knowledgeable about various domains can provide feedback helpful for debugging your learning strategies. However, to use these sources effectively you must first attempt to communicate to the expert what you have mastered. It is only then that the expert can evaluate your understanding of the subject and make suggestions that can be used to modify your learning strategies.

Imagine you meet someone who is an expert in a topic you are having difficulty learning. You could begin by explaining that you have been having difficulty knowing whether you learned adequately, and hence you need some feedback. Explain further that you have studied several concepts that seem to be important and that you would like help in deciding whether you have understood adequately. You can then tell the expert what the concepts are (veins and arteries) and ask the expert to ask you questions about the topics that beginners should be able to answer. This will allow you to discover quite quickly whether you are missing information the expert thinks is crucial. If you do this for a number of concepts, you will also develop an understanding of the expert's criteria for "adequate understanding."

This approach to debugging takes commitment and preparation, and you must be brave enough to risk making mistakes in front of others. Nevertheless, it is an efficient and valuable way to learn. Furthermore, we are confident that most instructors and experts will respect your motivation and maturity. They know everyone makes errors. They also know effective learners try to make them only once, and they try to make them *before* an exam or meeting rather than during those activities. By identifying and defining problems beforehand, you can avoid embarrassments and inefficiencies later on.

SUMMARY

The major theme of this chapter was that the strategies necessary to learn with understanding differ from those necessary to merely memorize information. Effective learners must be able to *identify* and *define* problems with their ability to understand the significance of new information ("This passage seems arbitrary; there must be a reason arteries are elastic and veins are not," and "The salesman has not explained why this new type of scissors has the shape it does"). Effective learners can then *explore* strategies that permit an understanding of the significance or relevance of information. In addition, they *actively* apply particular strategies and *look* at the effects. If comprehension problems are still identified, they enter the IDEAL cycle once again.

Several characteristics of the IDEAL problem solver were emphasized in our discussion. First, we noted that successful problem solving requires knowledge of appropriate concepts. For example, it would be difficult to understand the letter about Sally (the one who let the gophers loose to get her neighbor to move) without knowledge of what a neighbor is and why it might be difficult to get rid of one. Similarly, the ability to fully comprehend the letter about the NASA scientist (the one who argued that data from a recent space voyage questioned existing theories about the formation of the universe) requires knowledge of astronomy. Effective problem solving involves more than such skills as "the ability to make inferences." Without an adequate knowledge base, appropriate inferences cannot be made.

Second, we emphasized that novices who are attempting to learn about a new area of knowledge frequently confront the problem of learning about facts and relationships that seem arbitrary and hence confusing. Thus, they may see no reason why an artery should be elastic or nonelastic, thick or thin. We noted that one approach to the problem of learning arbitrary relationships is to use such memory techniques as interactive images. An alternate approach is to attempt to understand why things are the way they are; for example, to search for relationships between the structure and function of veins and arteries, types of American Indian houses, types of scissors, and so on. Such strategies are often more complex and difficult than those that permit us to merely memorize information. Nevertheless, the extra effort is usually worthwhile because concepts that are understood can function as conceptual tools that allow us to solve subsequent problems. Thus, the person who understands why veins and arteries are constructed as they are is in a much better position to approach the problem of designing an artificial artery. The mere memorization of facts rarely results in useful conceptual tools.

A third point emphasized involved the concept of levels of precision. Our knowledge of various concepts (airports, gold, or veins and arteries) may vary in precision. The level of precision necessary depends on the contexts in which our knowledge must be used. For example, a child may have only a vague knowledge of airports and yet be able to use this knowledge to understand the statement, "Aunt Jane is coming so we need to go to the airport." In other contexts, however (in the context of statements that presuppose knowledge of metal detectors), a cursory knowledge of airports will not permit comprehension.

Fourth, we discussed the problem of assessing our current levels of understanding. Effective learners attempt to anticipate ways they must use information (to anticipate the questions on a test or the questions that will be asked after a talk). This provides guidance about the level of precision of information that must be acquired. Nevertheless, it is frequently impossible to predict with accuracy the types of problems (test questions or questions following a talk) we ultimately will face. As a result, we will sometimes be unable to answer questions and will make mistakes. Effective learners try to learn from their mistakes; they develop strategies that enable them to avoid making similar mistakes in the future. The development of these "debugging skills" is an extremely important aspect of learning to learn.

EXERCISES

Try to activate concepts that make the sentences below comprehensible.

1. The breakfast was delicious because the thread was sticky.
2. The stream of water stopped because it started raining.
3. The car moved because the coin was bent.
4. The streak blocked the light.

Listed below are some patterns of words that would be relatively easy to memorize. However, it is more interesting to try to understand them. For example, the pattern "you just me" can be interpreted as "just between you and me."

5. $\dfrac{\text{wear}}{\text{thermal}}$

6. sttheory

7. 0

B.S.

M.S.

Ph.D.

D.D.

8. /r/e/a/d/i/n/g/

9. wheather

10. Read the instructions provided below for operating a pencil sharpener.

After selecting the proper size of guide hole, turn the handle clockwise.

Evaluate the adequacy of these instructions for people who have never seen or used a pencil before. Rewrite the instructions to resolve these deficiencies.

Imagine that a child reads a passage containing some facts about camels.

They have special eyelids that can cover their eyes yet still let in some light.
They can close their nose passages.
They have thick hair around their ear openings.

11. What might you do to help the child understand the significance or relevance of these facts rather than merely memorize them?

12. How might children's abilities to understand the significance of these facts allow them to better understand other events they read about?

13. A spy wants to hide a roll of secret film he has reduced to ⅛ inch in diameter and 2¼ inches long. Looking at his bookshelf, he notices the two-volume desk-top encyclopedia series illustrated below.

Using a drill that is ¼ inch in diameter, the spy begins on page 1 of volume 1 and drills straight through to the last page of volume 2. Assume that the cover on each book is ¼ inch thick and that each book without its cover is 1 inch thick. Is the hole long enough to hold the roll of film? How long is the hole?

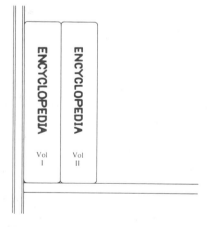

NOTES

[1]This passage was adapted from one that was written originally by Nancy McCarrell.

[2]This passage is from J. R. Mehan, Tale-spin, an interactive program that writes stories, *Proceedings from the Fifth International Joint Conference on Artificial Intelligence*, 1977, pp. 91–98.

[3]Additional discussion of the importance of previously acquired knowledge for learning can be found in: J. D. Bransford and M. K. Johnson, Contextual prerequisites for understanding: Some investigations of comprehension and recall, *Journal of Verbal Learning and Verbal Behavior, 11,* 717–726, 1972. J. J. Franks, J. J. Bransford, and P. M. Auble, The activation and utilization of knowledge. In C. R. Puff (ed.), *Handbook of Research Methods in Human Memory and Cognition.* New York: Academic Press, K. Nelson, R. Fivush, J. Hudson, and J. Lucariello, Scripts and the development of memory. In M. T. H. Chi (Ed.), *Contributions to Human Development,* Vol. 9, *Trends in Memory Development Research.* New York: Kargar, 1983. R. C. Schank and R. P. Abelson, *Scripts, Plans, Goals and Understanding.* Hillsdale, N.J.: Erlbaum, 1977.

[4]This example is from A. M. Collins and M. R. Quillian, How to make a language user. In E. Tulving and W. Donaldson (Eds.), *Organization of Memory.* New York: Academic, 1972.

[5]From B. S. Stein and J. D. Bransford, Constraints on effective elaboration: Effects of precision and self-generation, *Journal of Verbal Learning and Verbal Behavior, 18,* 769–777, 1979.

[6]See C. E. Weinstein, Elaboration skills as a learning strategy. In H. F. O'Neil, Jr. (Ed.), *Learning Strategies.* New York: Academic, 1978.

[7]From J. D. Bransford and N. S. McCarrell, A sketch of a cognitive approach to comprehension. In W. Weimer and D. Palermo (Eds.), *Cognition and the Symbolic Processes.* Hillsdale, N.J.: Erlbaum, 1974.

[8]From J. D. Bransford, *Human Cognition: Learning, Understanding and Remembering.* Belmont, Calif.: Wadsworth, 1979.

[9]See J. D. Bransford, Schema activation versus schema acquisition. In R. Anderson, J. Osborn, and R. Tierney (Eds.), *Learning to Read in American Schools: Basal Readers and Content Texts.* Hillsdale, N.J.: Erlbaum, 1984.

[10]From R. S. Day, Teaching from notes: Some cognitive consequences. In W. J. McKeachie (Ed.), *New Directions for Teaching and Learning: Learning, Cognition and College Teaching.* San Francisco: Jossey-Bass, 1980. See also R. S. Day, *Cognition, Teaching and Learning,* in press.

[11]This example is discussed by G. A. Miller, Addendum to "Lexical Meaning." In J. F. Kavanagh and W. Strange (Eds.), *Speech and Language in the Laboratory, School and Clinic.* Cambridge, Mass.: MIT Press, 1978.

[12]From Bransford, 1984 (note 9).

[13]From Bransford, 1979 (note 8).

[14]Additional examples of access failure are discussed in: M. L. Gick and K. J. Holyoak, Analogical problem solving, *Cognitive Psychology, 12,* 306–355, 1980; G. A. Perfetto, J. D. Bransford, and J. J. Franks, Constraints on access in a problem solving context, *Memory and Cognition, 11,* 24–31, 1983.

[15]A discussion of the general importance of debugging can be found in S. Papert, *Mindstorms: Children, Computers and Powerful Ideas.* New York: Basic Books, 1980.

SUGGESTED READINGS

Theoretically Oriented Readings

Anderson, R. C., The role of reader's schema in comprehension, learning and memory. In R. Anderson, J. Osborn, and R. Tierney (Eds.), *Learning to Read in American Schools: Basal Readers and Content Texts*. Hillsdale, N.J.: Erlbaum, 1984.

Asher, J., Fear of foreign languages, *Psychology Today*, August, 1981.

Bransford, J. D., B. S. Stein, N. J. Vye, J. J. Franks, P. M. Auble, K. J. Mezynski, and G. A. Perfetto, Differences in approaches to learning: An overview, *Journal of Experimental Psychology: General, 111*, 390–398, 1982.

Bransford, J. D., N. J. Vye, L. T. Adams, and G. A. Perfetto, Learning skills and the acquisition of knowledge. In R. Glaser and A. Lesgold (Eds.), *Handbook of Psychology and Education*. Hillsdale, N.J.: Erlbaum, in press.

Brown, A. L., J. D. Bransford, R. A. Ferrara, and J. C. Campione, Learning, remembering and understanding. In J. H. Flavell and E. M. Markman (Eds.), *Carmichael's Manual of Child Psychology*, Vol. 1. New York: Wiley, 1983.

Brown, A. L., and J. S. DeLoache, Skills, plans and self-regulation. In R. S. Siegler (Ed.), *Children's Thinking: What Develops?* Hillsdale, N.J.: Erlbaum, 1978.

Chase, W. G., and H. A. Simon, Perception in chess, *Cognitive Psychology, 4*, 55–81, 1973.

Glenberg, A. M., A. C. Wilkinson, and W. Epstein, The illusion of knowing: Failure in the self-assessment of comprehension, *Memory and Cognition, 10*, 597–602, 1982.

Harris, R. J., Comprehension of pragmatic implications in advertising, *Journal of Applied Psychology, 62*, 603–608, 1977.

Markman, E. M., Realizing that you don't understand: A preliminary investigation, *Child Development, 48*, 986–992, 1977.

Perfetto, G. A., J. D. Bransford, and J. F. Franks, Constraints on access in a problem solving context, *Memory and Cognition, 11*, 24–31, 1983.

Spilich, G. J., G. T. Vesonder, H. L. Chiesi, and J. F. Voss, Text processing of domain-related information for individuals with high and low domain knowledge, *Journal of Verbal Learning and Verbal Behavior, 18*, 275–290, 1979.

5

INTELLIGENT CRITICISM

The most important factor in the training of good mental habits consists in acquiring the attitude of suspended conclusion, and in mastering the various methods of searching for new materials to corroborate or to refute the first suggestions that occur.

John Dewey[1]

Our discussion in Chapter 4 emphasized strategies for acquiring information from others and from such sources as books, lectures, and personal conversations. Clearly, it is important to be able to learn what others have said and discovered. Nevertheless, it is equally if not more important to develop the skills necessary to analyze ideas and discoveries critically. Whether we are lawyers, scientists, business executives, or consumers, we must learn to evaluate the barrage of claims and arguments that confronts us every day.

In his book, *Till Death Us Do Part*, Bugliosi describes a famous murder trial held in California.[2] Since there were no eyewitnesses, the trial was based solely on circumstantial evidence. Near the end of the trial, the defense lawyer tries to convince the jury that the defendant is innocent. He reminds the jury that the trial was based on circumstantial evidence and then argues that a trial of this type is like a chain. A chain is only as strong as its weakest link, and the defense lawyer argues that the jury needs a strong chain to convict the defendant. He then proceeds to show that there is not simply one weak link, there are several weak links in the chain.

Imagine you are the prosecuting attorney in this trial. You speak to the jury after the defense finishes its presentation. To convince the jury the defendant is guilty, you need more than the skills necessary to comprehend what the defense lawyer has said to the jury. You also need the skills necessary to criticize the defense lawyer's argument and to communicate your ideas in a clear and persuasive manner.

There are a number of ways to criticize arguments. One is to focus on factual accuracy. For example, the defense attorney may have stated (erroneously) that a jury cannot reach a guilty verdict if there is nothing but circumstantial evidence. Given this argument, you could challenge the accuracy of the defense attorney's facts.

A second way to criticize an argument is to demonstrate that someone's reasoning is not logical and consistent. A person may begin with accurate facts but the conclusion that he or she wants to draw may be invalid. For example, that the defendant drinks beer yet a wine bottle was found near the victim does not prove the defendant is innocent.

A third way to attack an argument is to question basic assumptions (implicit or explicit definitions of a problem). People's facts may be correct and their arguments may be sound *given* that you grant them various assumptions. Frequently, however, the creative person can come up with a set of assumptions that differ from those that have been made previously. In the California trial, for example, the prosecuting attorney (Bugliosi) questioned a basic assumption made by the defense attorney: Bugliosi argued that trials based on circumstantial evidence are analogous to a *rope* rather than a chain. A rope is composed of a number of independent strands; several of these can break without having much effect on the overall strength of the rope. Bugliosi acknowledged that there were indeed a few questionable strands, but he emphasized that the rest of the evidence was more than strong enough to convict the defendant. (For whatever it's worth, Bugliosi won the case.)

Note that the processes involved in criticism are consistent with the IDEAL perspective. Thus, you may first *identify* the existence of a problem with someone's argument ("something seems to be wrong here") and then try to *define* the problem more precisely. Imagine that you first define the problem as "factual inaccuracy"; this invites the *exploration* of various strategies for verifying the evidence presented. By *actively* using a strategy (reading information in a textbook) you can then *look* at the effects. Assume that the effects are negative, that is, that you are unable to show the argument is factually inaccurate. This may lead you to reenter the IDEAL cycle and redefine the nature of the problem; for example, the argument's conclusions do not follow logically or the argument is based on assumptions that do not necessarily hold.

As noted earlier, the skills necessary to critically evaluate arguments and to view them from alternate perspectives (from the perspective of a rope rather than a chain) are not restricted to courts of law. Such skills are important in a variety of contexts. For instance, we need to evaluate claims made by various advertisers (for example, "This year's model of our car is 20 percent more fuel efficient"). These claims, as well as many others, often involve "statistical" and "scientific" arguments that are much weaker than they may appear at first glance.

The major goal of this chapter is to explore strategies for finding and correcting flaws in arguments. We focus on the three general classes of strategies mentioned earlier, namely, (1) evaluating factual claims, (2) looking for flaws in logic and logical consistency, and (3) questioning assumptions that form the basis of the argument.

THE ANALYSIS OF FACTUAL CLAIMS

Imagine that you win $10,000 in a contest and want to invest the money. An investment counselor offers you a once-in-a-lifetime opportunity: He knows someone who is willing to part with an ancient coin for a fraction of what it is worth. You examine the coin and observe that it does indeed look authentic. The investment counselor emphasizes that the date stamped on it, 42 B.C., indicates that it is very old and hence should be worth at least twice as much as the price you are asked to pay (which is $9100). He also explains that the seller is willing to part with the coin at this low price only because she needs the money immediately and because it usually takes about a month to sell antique coins for the price they are worth. Would you buy the coin? Why or why not?

If you decided to buy the coin you also bought a faulty argument. One of the facts used to support the claim that the coin is ancient cannot be true. In order to stamp a coin 42 B.C. the coin maker would have had to know in advance not only the exact year of the birth of Christ (note that B.C. stands for "before Christ"), but also that this would be a basis for dating in the future. Since this is extremely doubtful, it seems clear the coin is a fake.

Note that the claim, "This coin was minted in 42 B.C." is not necessarily false. It is possible to have found a coin this old. The problem with the coin argument presented above is not the claim itself, it is *the evidence for the claim* (the evidence was the date printed on the coin). Geologists and archeologists make claims about the age of various entities (fossils and skeletons), but they do so by providing evidence for their claims that seem reasonable given current scientific knowledge (they often use radioactive "tracers" to date various entities). Effective critics pay careful attention to the nature of the evidence upon which claims are based.[3]

Evaluating Invited Inferences

You can learn a lot about the importance of searching for the basis of claims by studying advertisements. By law, advertisers cannot lie; for example, it would be illegal to advertise that coins with 42 B.C. stamped on them are authentic. Nevertheless, advertisements are often designed to prompt us to make "invited inferences" about messages that, from a logical and scientific perspective, do not follow.

Consider the following claim.

Scientific studies show that our brand (brand A) is unsurpassed by any other brand on the market.

How do you interpret this statement? Many people assume that brand A has been shown to be superior to other brands. This is only an invited inference, however. Legally, *unsurpassed* means that the researchers have found no differences in the effectiveness of brand A versus other brands.

Here is another example of a possible claim.

Dogs prefer our brand of food by a ratio of 2 to 1.

What is missing here is any explicit mention of what was used as a comparison. The advertised brand could have been compared to uncooked cabbage, for example. Such information is often deleted in the hope that the consumer will make the invited inference that a reasonable comparison group was used.

Look at the graph in Figure 5.1 that appeared in an advertisement for a new weight-reducing product. Many people who see this graph conclude that, by using the product advertised, they could lose a large amount of weight in a short period of time. However, if you examine the graph more thoroughly you will notice that the units of weight loss and time have not been specified clearly. The conclusion that the product is highly effective is only an invited inference. It is possible, for example, that in actual tests the new product could have produced a reduction of only 1 ounce during a period of 6 months. When analyzing graphs and charts it is always important to check the units of measurement to evaluate the claims being made.

Scientific "Facts"

It would be unfair to give the impression that the purpose of all modern advertisements is to mislead people. Many are designed to inform us of products that are quite good. In addition, misleading arguments are by no means confined to the field of advertisement. Arguments found in newspapers, textbooks, conversations, and even in scientific articles may be based on questionable facts.

Figure 5.1
A graph illustrating weight loss as a function of time.

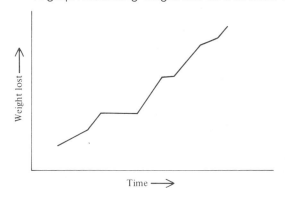

The following set of data represents the number of deaths per million boat passengers that occurred in 1973[4]:

Canoe (motor)	0.14
Canoe (no motor)	1.66
Sailboat (auxiliary motor)	0.44
Sailboat (no motor)	0.52

When asked to draw conclusions on the basis of these data, many people state there are fewer deaths in boats with motors because motors provide a safety factor, and they go on to explain why. For example, a motor provides an alternative means of transportation in case of accidents like a broken arm or a torn sail; furthermore, a motor allows one to travel faster and hence avoid such problems as storms and high winds. Overall, many people state that the preceding data show that *boats with motors are safer than boats without motors*. This statement, therefore, seems to constitute a fact.

If you think about it you will realize there are problems with this "factual" statement. The reason is there are many differences between boats with and without motors other than the presence or absence of motors. For example, white-water canoers would never use a motor, whereas people who canoe on calm lakes (which generally are safer than fast-moving streams) would be much more likely to use a motor. With respect to sailboats, only the larger craft (those less likely to capsize) are likely to have motors. In addition, people who are inexperienced sailors may be more likely to have the smaller, less stable boats. Given these considerations, it is questionable that motors themselves are the reason for differences in safety. Indeed, in many situations (canoeing on fast rivers or sailing a small boat on a windy lake) it seems likely that the presence of a motor could make the boat less safe.

Many types of claims are based on data similar to that of the boat example:

At a meeting of educators, a committee chairman reported on a study that had just been completed. Questionnaires had been sent to teachers; two of the questions asked were: (a) How much do you like computers? and (b) How much experience have you had with computers? The data showed that people who said that they had had more experience with computers were the ones who liked them better. Based on these data, the chairman made the following conclusion: "We can therefore see that the more that people are exposed to computers the more that they will like them." Do the data support this factual claim?

It is quite possible that exposure to computers increases the degree to which people like them. Nevertheless, the data presented by the committee chair do not really support this claim. The chair is suggesting that experiences with computers *cause* increases in liking. The opposite relationship is also possible, namely, that people who feel they like computers are likely to seek opportunities to learn about them; hence, they report having more experience with them. In this case, the degree of liking "causes" the contact with computers.

The data do not allow us to say whether liking causes contact with computers, whether contact causes liking, whether each affects the other, and so forth. The reason is that the data involve only correlations between two variables. Evidence for a correlation between variables (liking and contact with computers, or motors on boats and safety) does not indicate which variable causes the other. Indeed, both might be caused by a third variable. For example, it is not difficult to find a positive correlation between increases in teacher's salaries and increases in alcohol consumption. This doesn't necessarily mean that teachers used their raises to buy liquor. Instead, the correlation is probably due to some third variable that affects raises as well as consumption. A likely candidate would be an increase in the general economy; this could allow schools to pay teachers more and increase the probability that nearly all other people had extra money to spend.

The Importance of Experimental Analysis

The preceding discussion emphasizes a common mistake in reasoning: *Correlational data are often interpreted as indicating cause and effect.* Nevertheless, there are times when it is valid to conclude that one thing is caused by or affected by another. It is important to understand the nature of the evidence necessary to make such claims. For example, what kinds of data provide convincing evidence that, as people's contacts with computers increase, they like computers more?[5]

One approach to the preceding problem is as follows. Imagine that 100 people are randomly assigned to two groups (random assignment means that each person has an equally likely chance to be in either group, one might put each person's name in a hat and assign the first name drawn to group 1, the second drawn to group 2, the third drawn to group 3, and so forth). If assignment to groups is truly random, we would expect that, on the average, members of each group would have had an approximately equal amount of experience with computers (many in each group would probably have had no experience) and would like computers approximately equally well.

Assume that all people in the experiment receive a questionnaire asking about (1) the amount of experience with computers they have had and (2) the degree to which they like computers. We could then arrange it so that members of the two groups receive different experiences. For example, assume that people in group 1 work with computers for 1 hour per day for a period of 2 weeks; people in group 2 (the control group) do not work with computers. At the end of the experiment we give everyone another questionnaire that asks them to rate the degree to which they like computers. If experiences with computers increase the degree to which people like them, we should find that people who received computer training increased their liking for computers, whereas people in the control group did not. Such data would allow us to conclude that an increase in experiences with computers increases the degree to which people report liking them.

Note, however, that even the preceding claim can be an overgeneralization. It may imply that experiences with computers affect *all* people positively. Furthermore, it suggests that any type of experience with computers (learning to program in BASIC versus playing video games) may be equally likely to increase liking. A more finely tuned experiment could be conducted as follows. People are first assigned to groups on the basis of how much they think they will like computers (a great deal, pretty much, or not at all). Half the members of each group could then be given experiences with computers, whereas the other half would act as a control (no computer experience). After 2 weeks, people would again be asked to rate the degree to which they like computers.

Given this type of design, it is possible to assess whether experiences with computers affect different groups in different ways. For example, people who thought they would like computers "a great deal" or "pretty much" may increase their liking after experiences with computers, whereas people who felt that they would not like computers could actually decrease their liking after working with computers. However, this pattern of results may occur only for some types of experiences with computers (such as learning to program in BASIC) rather than others. In assessing a factual claim such as "greater experiences with computers increase people's liking for them," we therefore have to consider carefully the nature of the evidence. For example, we need to know something about who is being talked about, and we need information about the nature of the computer training people received.

Additional Illustrations of Factual Claims

Here are some additional examples of factual claims and descriptions of the evidence used to support them. See if you can spot problems with these claims. (Answers appear in Appendix E.)

> College professors are asked to indicate the degree to which they agree with various statements. One is, "Students who turn in papers that are typed tend to get higher grades than students who do not type their papers." Most of the professors surveyed indicate that they agree with this statement. On the basis of these data, a typewriter company recommends that students learn to type so that they can get better grades. Do the data support this conclusion? Why or why not?

> Sid Slye wants to sell you a special gas-saving device for your car for only $100. "How do I know it works?" you ask. "That's easy," says Sid. "I have one on my car and it gets 45 miles per gallon. My other car doesn't have one, and it gets only 25 miles per gallon." Is this enough information to convince you that the device works?

> The number of people who send in a $1 rebate form is found to be related to their average annual income in the following manner.

Income	Number of people
Less than $20,000	10,000
$20,000–$40,000	7000
Over $40,000	4000

Can you conclude from these data that people who make more money are less likely to worry about collecting rebates? Why or why not?

THE LOGIC OF ARGUMENTS

In the preceding discussion we emphasized situations in which the "facts" used to support arguments were questionable. For example, the claim, "people should be encouraged to put motors on their canoes," might be based on the "fact," "canoes with motors have been shown to be safer than canoes without motors." As noted earlier, however, this claim is not supported by the data that were presented. It is therefore important to analyze the nature of the evidence used to support various factual claims.

Another way to analyze arguments is to assume that we begin with a fact that is accurate (a premise) and ask how we can use it to make a "logical" point. That is, what must we do to ensure that our conclusions follow logically from a set of premises or facts?[6]

Here is a claim that seems to be supported by the study of history. "Many new scientific theories that later proved to be valid were first ridiculed." In medicine, for example, Pasteur's idea that diseases were transmitted by germs too small to see with the naked eye was considered by many to be a totally unrealistic view.

How might the fact, "Many valid scientific theories were at first ridiculed," be used in an argument? Imagine that you create a theory criticized by several other scientists. A reporter suggests you should give up in the face of such criticism. A possible response would be, "Look, history shows that many valid theories were at first ridiculed. Therefore, the fact that some people ridicule my theory does not prove it is wrong."[7]

Here is another possible response to the reporter. "Look, history shows that many valid theories were at first ridiculed. Therefore, the fact that my theory has been ridiculed shows it is correct."

You probably feel much more comfortable with the first argument than the second. Only in the first argument does the conclusion seem to follow from the fact (premise) from which the argument began. These two arguments illustrate a type of reasoning known as *syllogistic* reasoning.

Argument 1
Some theories that have been criticized have turned out to be valid (major premise).
My theory is being criticized (minor premise).
Therefore, it could turn out to be valid (conclusion).

Argument 2
Some theories that have been criticized have turned out to be valid (major premise).
My theory is being criticized (minor premise).
Therefore, it is valid (conclusion).

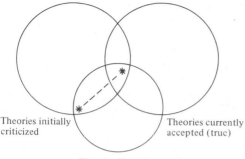

Theories initially
criticized

Theories currently
accepted (true)

Theories like mine

Figure 5.2
Note that "my theory" could fall into either of the two places in the diagram
marked by asterisks. If it falls into the space designated by the asterisk on the left,
the theory would not be currently accepted as true.

Figure 5.2 represents the relationship among theories that are initially criticized,
theories that are accepted, and theories like yours using Venn diagrams. These
diagrams are a powerful tool for analyzing arguments in detail. The use of Venn
diagrams makes it clear that the second argument presented above is not logically
sound.

Imagine that the facts of history were somewhat different. For example,
imagine that, "All (rather than some) theories that later turned out to be valid
were criticized initially." Could one now conclude that criticism of one's theory
proves that it is true? The answer is no; many invalid theories could also

Figure 5.3
Note that "my theory" could fall into either of the two places in the diagram
marked by asterisks. If it falls into the space designated by the asterisk on the left,
the theory would not be currently accepted as true.

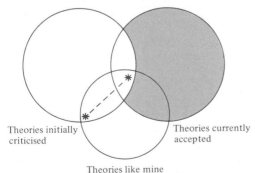

Theories initially
criticised

Theories currently
accepted

Theories like mine
(Shaded areas denote no members)

have been criticized initially. This is illustrated by the Venn diagrams shown in Figure 5.3.

Consider one more possible "historical fact," namely, "All new theories that initially are criticized turn out to be valid." Given this premise, you would be in a much stronger position to make the argument that the presence of criticism suggests your theory is valid (see Figure 5.4). Note, however, that the historical fact upon which this argument is based is mythical rather than true.

If-Then Arguments

Many arguments we make follow an "if-then" structure. You are undoubtedly familiar with a very simple if-then statement known as a guarantee: "If you are not satisfied with our product, [then] we will refund your money." Another example may be found in your insurance policy: "If you have a car accident, we will pay for damages." The if-then statement is used to describe a relationship between two events; it tells us what should happen if certain events occur (we will be able to get our money back if we are not satisfied with the product). Each if-then argument includes what is called an *antecedent* (if you are not satisfied with our product) and what is called a *consequent* (we will refund your money). When we are given a clear if-then statement and we find the antecedent condition to be true (we are not satisfied with the product), we can rightfully expect the consequent condition to also be true (we will be able to get our money back). ˙

If-then statements occur in a variety of settings. For example, assume once again you are a lawyer in a trial. This time you are a defense lawyer. You have established that your client (the defendant) has an ironclad alibi for 9 to 12 A.M. on the day of the murder. You might therefore want to make the argument, "If the

Figure 5.4
Note that "my theory" must be accepted because, in this instance, all theories that were initially criticized are currently accepted as true.

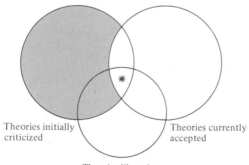

Theories initially criticized

Theories currently accepted

Theories like mine

(Shaded areas denote no members)

Note that "my theory" must be accepted because, in this instance, all theories that were initially criticized are currently accepted as true.

murder occurred between 9 and 12 A.M., my client is innocent." The form of this argument is, "If A, then B."

Assume that the time of the murder is established as 10 A.M. Your argument would then be, "If the murder occurred between 9 and 12 A.M., then my client is innocent (because of the airtight alibi). The murder did occur during this time; therefore, my client is innocent." The general form of this argument is, "If A, then B; A, therefore B." This is a valid argument to make.

Suppose we try to reverse the argument. That is, if the client is truly innocent, can we conclude that the murder therefore took place at the time when he had an alibi, that is, between 9 and 12 A.M.? The answer is no; the murder could have taken place at a variety of times. The form of this argument is, "If A, then B; B, therefore A." Philosophers refer to this form of argument as the fallacy of affirming the consequent (where A is the antecedent and B is the consequent). This is an invalid argument form.

It is instructive to note that many tests of theories are of the form, "If A (this theory is correct), then B (the following results should be obtained)." For example, a theory of the effects of imagery on memory might predict that people who form images of information to be remembered will remember more than people who do not form images (see Chapter 3 for a discussion of imagery). Assume that this experiment is conducted, and the prediction holds. Can we conclude that the imagery theory is correct? Note that the form of this argument would be "If A (the imagery theory is correct), then B (the group told to image should remember more); B (the imagery group did remember more), therefore A (the imagery theory is correct)." As noted above, this is an invalid form of argument that involves the fallacy of affirming the consequent. It is for this reason that logicians caution that one cannot prove a theory is correct. Instead, one can only say "These results are consistent with the theory," or "These results provide support for the theory."

There are two more if-then argument forms; these can be illustrated by returning to the trial example. One is, if A, then B; not A, therefore not B. In the context of the trial this translates as follows. If the murder occurred between 9 and 12 A.M., then my client is innocent. The murder did not occur during this time; therefore, my client is not innocent. This is not an argument you would want to make as a defense lawyer. Fortunately, it also involves what philosophers call the fallacy of denying the antecedent and is an invalid argument form. In the case of the client, it is possible that he had been fishing alone at a remote cabin, for example, and no one else may have known it; hence, he could not prove that he was not at the scene of the murder when the victim was killed. Nevertheless, the absence of an alibi does not prove the presence of guilt.

The fourth form of if-then argument is, "If the murder occurred between 9 and 12 A.M., then my client is innocent. My client is not innocent, therefore the murder did not occur between 9 and 12 A.M." Although as a defense lawyer you might be reluctant to admit that your client is not innocent, the form of this argument is valid. The form is: "If A, then B; not B, therefore not A." Note that it is this form of argument that can be used to disprove a theory; that is, one can argue, "If this theory is true, then the following experimental result should be obtained. The result was not obtained; therefore (assuming that the study was carried out appropriately) the theory cannot be true." We will discuss limitations on this form of reasoning later.

The four basic forms of if-then arguments are presented in Table 5.1. You might want to try them with a different set of arguments. For example, consider the premise, "If it is a triangle, then it is red." Now try to answer the following questions: If the shape is not a triangle, it is not red? If it is not red, it is not a triangle? The argument forms can help you answer such questions. (See Appendix E for answers.)

The Consistency of Arguments

Another important feature of valid arguments is that they must be logically consistent. The search for inconsistencies plays an important role in a variety of areas. For example, consider once again a court of law. A witness may provide information inconsistent with his or her previous testimony, or may describe an event in a manner inconsistent with other people's testimony. The effective trial lawyer searches for such inconsistencies and makes sure the jury realizes they exist.

An advertisement that appeared in a Tennessee newspaper announced in bold type the following information: *A 45 piece tool set for only $10.00.* It went on to describe the pieces included: a hammer, a set of screwdrivers, a set of Allen wrenches, a retractable metal tape measure, and so forth. The offer seemed too good to be true. Further, the advertisement also described a free case that could be used to organize the tools and store them neatly. The next line in the advertisement stated that the case allowed you to fold the entire set of forty-five tools into just 1 inch of space.

For us, the information about storing the tools in 1 inch of space was totally

Table 5.1
Illustrations of Valid and Invalid Argument Forms

1. If A is true, then B is true. A is true. Therefore, B is true.	Valid
2. If A is true, then B is true. B is true. Therefore, A is true.	Not valid; fallacy of affirming the consequent
3. If A is true, then B is true. A is not true. Therefore, B is not true.	Not valid; fallacy of denying the antecedent
4. If A is true, then B is true. B is not true. Therefore, A is not true.	Valid

inconsistent with our previous assumptions about the set of tools, namely, that it included a full-sized hammer, a set of normal-sized screwdrivers, and so forth. We reasoned that either the tools must be minuscule (like a jeweler's screwdrivers and hammer) or the information about the 1 inch of storage space must have been a printing error. We are convinced the advertisement did not contain a printing error. Our bet is that the tools are indeed minuscule and worth considerably less than $10.00. Note that people who fail to see the inconsistency between their assumptions about the tools and the information about storage space will probably be angry when they receive the product. Nevertheless, the people who wrote the advertisement will undoubtedly claim that it told them what to expect; hence, it doesn't qualify as an instance of outright fraud.

The search for inconsistencies is also extremely important in science. In his book *Einstein's Universe,* for example, Nigel Calder discusses the search for black holes in space.[8] He describes the work of scientists who studied a galaxy of stars orbiting around the galaxy's center. The scientists knew that the speed of rotation of stars around a center or core depended on the mass of the core. The speed of the stars being studied was calculated and found to be extremely fast, approximately 250 miles per second. Based on this information it was possible to calculate the mass of the core necessary to sustain such movement. The calculations revealed that the mass must be enormous, roughly 5000 million times heavier than the sun.

Calder notes that the scientists also had access to an electronic light detector that allowed them to measure the amount of light (brightness) generated by the core being studied. He states, "If there was an enormous number of stars at the core, corresponding to the mass, the heart of the galaxy would be very bright indeed." (Note the if-then reasoning used.) When the scientists measured the light they found only a relatively faint glow rather than a dazzling display; the appearance of the core was therefore not what one would expect if it were composed of stars. Calder goes on to note that *information about the appearance of the core was inconsistent with calculations of the mass of the core, unless the core contained a black hole.* The detection of a possible inconsistency was therefore very important; it showed the need to postulate something, a black hole for example, that would allow the apparent inconsistency between the appearance and the mass of the core to be resolved.

THE ANALYSIS OF BASIC ASSUMPTIONS

Our previous discussion emphasized two general classes of strategies for detecting flaws in arguments: (1) evaluate the accuracy of factual claims, and (2) look for logical flaws and inconsistencies. The third strategy is to evaluate the assumptions on which an argument is based.

The evaluation of assumptions is especially important. For example, the fact that most arguments are based on sets of assumptions can make it difficult to apply some of the idealized rules of logic discussed earlier. Consider the premise, "If John invents a better mousetrap, he will become rich." From our previous discussion we can conclude it is not valid to say John must have invented a better mousetrap because he is now rich (that is, it is invalid to reason, "If A, then B; B is true, therefore A is true"). Similarly, we know from previous discussion it is not valid to say John will never become rich because he did not invent a better mousetrap (it is invalid to reason, "If A, then B; not A, therefore not B"). However, imagine it is some time in the future and we meet John and find he has never become very wealthy. Can we conclude that John never invented a better mousetrap? Logically, the form of the argument is, "If A, then B; not B, therefore not A." As discussed earlier, this is a valid argument form.

Note, however, that the logical forms discussed earlier represent idealized situations. In reality, John may have invented a better mousetrap but it may never have been marketed successfully, or people may have stopped buying mousetraps. What appears to be a valid argument logically (if A, then B; not B, therefore not A) has become an ambiguous situation in the real world. One reason for this ambiguity is that the truth of the relationship expressed in our premise ("If John invents a better mousetrap, then he will become rich") *depends on the existence of other conditions or assumptions* (mousetraps continue to be purchased, John employs a good marketing strategy, or John finds a financial backer). Generally, whenever we include events and observations from the real world in our relationships, we import additional assumptions or conditions that may not be immediately obvious. These assumptions have an important effect on the reasonableness of the arguments we make.[9]

Assumptions and Inconsistencies

Basic assumptions must also be analyzed to evaluate the existence of inconsistencies. For example, anyone familiar with political debates has probably witnessed at least one situation in which two politicians present facts or statistics that seem to contradict one another. How is it possible for such inconsistencies to occur? Although politicians may occasionally make factual errors, more often than not the collection of facts involves subjective judgments or assumptions. For example, two politicians may argue about changes in workers' income during one politician's administration. The incumbent may argue that workers' wages increased 30 percent during this administration. The challenger may argue that workers' salaries actually declined by 5 percent during the same period. Neither of the statistics cited by the politicians may be wrong; they may simply be based on different assumptions. Thus, the challenger may have taken into account the rate of inflation during the survey period and adjusted wages accordingly while the incumbent did not.

Earlier, we discussed several examples in which an apparent inconsistency was resolved by making particular assumptions. For example, the inconsistency between a set of forty-five full-sized tools and the fact that they could be stored in 1 inch of space was resolved by assuming that the tools were in fact miniature rather than full sized. Similarly, we discussed Calder's description of scientists studying a galaxy and its core. They found that the appearance of the core (the degree of light emitted) seemed inconsistent with the calculations of its mass *unless* they made assumptions about the existence of a black hole. Much scientific theorizing involves the creation of new concepts and theories that resolve inconsistencies that seem to exist.

Everyday comprehension also involves assumptions that can resolve inconsistencies. Here are some simple statements that appear to contain inconsistencies unless you make appropriate assumptions.[10]

The floor was dirty because Sally used the mop.
John is able to come to the party tonight because his car broke down.
The dress wrinkled because Jill ironed it.

Examples of possible assumptions for these statements appear in Appendix E. Consider the following problem.

A woman called the police and stated that she had just murdered her husband by shooting him. The police went to the house and found that, sure enough, the man had just been shot. Despite the woman's fingerprints on the gun plus her testimony (she also passed a lie detector test that indicated she was not lying), the courts were unable to punish her by putting her in jail or sentencing her to death. Why?

Note that, at first glance, this problem seems to involve an inconsistency between what we know about murder and what we know about the law. Most people try to resolve this apparent inconsistency by making assumptions, such as "She really didn't do it," "It was an accident," or "She is insane so she cannot be prosecuted." However, in this problem the woman *did* commit the crime, she is perfectly sane, and the reason for not being able to jail her or put her to death has nothing to do with little technicalities in the law (for example, because the police failed to read her her rights). See if you can come up with an assumption that makes the apparent inconsistency disappear. (The answer appears in Appendix E.)

The Reasonableness of Assumptions

The fact that assumptions play such an important role in evaluating facts, logical arguments, and apparent inconsistencies has an obvious but important implication: We must evaluate carefully the reasonableness of the assumptions that form the basis of arguments. At the beginning of this chapter, for example, we discussed a murder trial in which the defense attorney made the assumption that a trial based on circumstantial evidence is like a chain. The remainder of his argument to the jury was consistent with the assumptions this analogy invokes. The prosecuting attorney made an alternate assumption, that a trial based on circumstantial evidence is like a rope rather than a chain. This allowed him to counter a number of points the defense attorney had made; for example, he argued that a few weak points in the overall testimony were not enough to indicate the defendant was innocent of the crime.

Many arguments are based on analogies. However, if the analogies are analyzed explicitly you may find that they are based on questionable assumptions. When left unanalyzed the arguments frequently seem to make sense, and we make assumptions and draw conclusions we probably should not draw.

Consider once again a situation discussed earlier. A scientist has created a new theory that is criticized; a reporter asks whether the theorist should give up in the face of this criticism. At this point the theorist may respond, "Your question reminds me of a story about Louis Pasteur. He was ridiculed unmercifully when he first suggested his germ theory of disease. As we all know, however, he got the last laugh."

What kind of argument is the theorist making by virtue of the reference to Pasteur? The argument might simply be, "That a new theory is ridiculed does not necessarily mean it is invalid." On the other hand, the theorist may purposely be keeping the argument ambiguous in the hope that listeners will make *invited inferences,* such as, "This situation is just like Pasteur's; hence, this new theory must be true." The theorists's reference to Pasteur illustrates a form of reasoning by analogy that is quite common in everyday situations. To evaluate such arguments, it is important to ask whether a particular analogy is appropriate, and if so, what the exact implications are supposed to be.

Consider a controversial topic, such as, "Should couples have sex before marriage?" A not uncommon enough reaction to this topic is to say something like "You wouldn't buy a car without taking it out for a test drive, would you?" Some people who hear this argument simply say, "Oh, yes, you have a point there." Others are much more critical of the argument and often become enraged at the inappropriateness of the analogy. For example, unlike a car, when you marry someone they don't become your property. In addition, problems that couples experience are usually two-way streets rather than always solely due to one's partner (analogous to one's car). Furthermore, people usually don't feel guilty after taking a test drive but many feel guilty after premarital sex. Even further, what if the couple didn't like their first "test drive"; should they therefore break up rather than try to work together to solve any problems? The car analogy does not suggest the idea of working together on anything.

You can undoubtedly find additional problems with the test drive analogy, but the basic point should be clear: The analogy carries with it a host of assumptions that are inappropriate and misleading. Assumptions have powerful effects on our reasoning; hence, it is important to analyze those we make as well as those others invite us to make.

SUMMARY

The major theme of this chapter was that effective problem solvers do not necessarily accept everything they hear or read. They are intelligent critics who can *identify* flaws in their own arguments as well as the arguments made by others. Once identified, they actively attempt to *define* the nature of the flaws, *explore* strategies for correcting them, *act* on the basis of particular strategies, and *look* at the effects. If the argument still seems faulty, they reenter the IDEAL cycle and try again.

Our discussion emphasized three general ways in which arguments may be faulty. One is that they may be based on inaccurate factual claims ("These data prove that more exposure to computers increases people's liking for them"). Note that people who make such claims are not necessarily trying to be misleading or dishonest. Instead, they frequently fail to realize their interpretations are in error.

A second reason arguments may be faulty involves the use of inappropriate logic. People may begin with an acceptable factual claim ("Many theories that later turned out to be true were at first ridiculed") yet end with a conclusion that does not follow from the facts ("Therefore, since my theory is being criticized, it must be true"). Similarly, people may make arguments that contain inconsistencies. When writing a paper, for example, an author may at first state that an historical figure never changed his mind about a particular issue yet later provide an example indicating that he did indeed change his mind.

A third reason for criticism involves the assumptions that form the basis of the argument. People's arguments will frequently seem valid if we grant them their initial assumptions ("Since war is inevitable, we should make the first strike"). However, once the basic assumptions are identified and questioned ("What makes you think that war is inevitable?"), arguments frequently lose their initial force. We also emphasized that the use of analogies and metaphors involves assumptions that may or may not be appropriate. Unless these are analyzed explicitly, they can lead us astray.

EXERCISES

1. What do you conclude from the statement, "Nine out of ten doctors surveyed recommended this product?"
2. What additional information would you want to know in order to evaluate the claim, "American school children scored lower on mathematics achievement tests than did children in all other industrialized countries." (Assume that all children were of comparable ages and all received comparable achievement tests.)
3. What are some possible problems with the following factual claim? "Our teachers are better than those at University X. Students who have graduated from our University average $10,000 more per year than do students who graduated from University X."
4. A school survey reveals that students who have computers at home earn significantly better grades than students who do not have computers at home. Should the school recommend that parents buy their children computers?
5. In 1927, Elton Mayo began a study at his plant to investigate the effects of illumination intensity on worker productivity. One of the findings in that investigation revealed that, when the illumination level was increased at the plant, productivity went up. If you were the plant manager, would you increase the lighting provided for workers at the plant? Why or why not?
6. If all men in Scottberg live on Gorkey Street and no people who live on Gorkey Street love strawberry pie, can we logically conclude that some men who live in Scottberg love strawberry pie?

7. If all xenos are oxons and some oxons are red, can one conclude that all xenos are red?

8. If all xenos are oxons and all zeeps are xenos, can one conclude that all zeeps are oxons?

9. Assume that the following is true: "If I go to the party I cannot do my homework." If I did not do my homework, can one conclude I went to the party?

10. To test a theory that RNA is used to store information in the brain, scientists injected twenty people with RNA. They found that the twenty people performed no better on a memory test after they were injected with RNA than before they were injected with RNA. Have they disproved the theory that RNA is used to store information in the brain?

11. Read the following game rules and then answer the questions below.

This is a two-player game. Each player starts at opposite corners of a checkerboard. The players move around the outside edge only. The object of the game is to reach the other player's corner first. Each player rolls the dice, and the player with the highest roll goes first. This player also picks a direction, either clockwise or counterclockwise. The other player must move in the opposite direction. On each turn the dice are rolled and the player with the highest roll advances one square on the board. The other player does not move on that turn. Players cannot occupy the same square at the same time.

a. Does the player who moves first have an advantage?
b. How long would the average game last?
c. If you played 100 games, how many would you expect to win?

Many riddles involving logical reasoning center around the problem of differentiating a liar from one who tells the truth. Here are two.

12. You are at a crossroads and need directions about which path to take to the nearest town, but you don't know if the only person there to help you is a liar or truthful. If he is truthful he will always answer truthfully; if he is a liar, he will always answer untruthfully. Using only one question, how can you find out which path is correct?

13. There are two brothers, one of whom always tells the truth and the other always lies. The truthful brother is very knowledgeable and always answers correctly; the liar is very poorly informed and always thinks things are just the opposite of how they really are. Since the liar is both poorly informed and lies, he will usually answer questions identically to his brother. For example, the liar would answer yes to the question, "Is two plus two equal to four?" because he thinks that $2 + 2$ is not equal to 4, but lies about it. Can you ask one question requiring a yes or no answer that will tell you which brother you are talking to?

NOTES

[1]J. Dewey, *How We Think*. Boston: D. C. Heath, 1910.

[2]V. Bugliosi, *'Till Death Us Do Part*. New York: Bantam, 1979.

[3]See D. Huff, *How to Lie with Statistics*. New York: W. W. Norton, 1954.

[4]These data are from the National Safety Council, 1973.

[5]More extensive discussion of experimental designs can be found in: A. Myers, *Experimental Psychology*. New York: D. Van Nostrand, 1976. D. Radner, and M. Radner,

Science and Unreason. Belmont, Calif.: Wadsworth, 1982. C. L. Sheridan, *Fundamentals of Experimental Psychology* (2nd Ed.). New York: Holt, Rinehart & Winston, 1976.

[6]More extensive discussions of reasoning can be found in: M. Scriven, *Reasoning.* New York: McGraw-Hill, 1976. S. Toulmin, *The Uses of Argument.* Cambridge, England: Cambridge University Press, 1958. S. Toulmin, R. Rieke, and A. Janik, *An Introduction to Reasoning.* New York: Macmillan, 1979.

[7]See M. Gardner, *Fads and Fallacies in the Name of Science.* New York: Dover, 1957.

[8]N. Calder, *Einstein's Universe.* New York: Penguin, 1980.

[9]T. Kuhn, *The Structure of Scientific Revolutions.* Chicago: University of Chicago Press, 1962.

[10]These examples are from J. D. Bransford and N. S. McCarrell, A sketch of a cognitive approach to comprehension. In W. Weimer and D. Palermo (Eds.), *Cognition and the Symbolic Processes.* Hillsdale, N.J.: Erlbaum, 1974.

SUGGESTED READINGS

Practically Oriented Readings

Anderson, B. F., *The Complete Thinker.* Englewood Cliffs, N.J.: Prentice-Hall, 1980, Chapter 3, on reasoning.

Beardsley, M. C., *Thinking Straight: Principles of Reasoning for Readers and Writers.* Englewood Cliffs, N.J.: Prentice-Hall, 1950.

Campbell, S. K., *Flaws and Fallacies in Statistical Thinking.* Englewood Cliffs, N.J.: Prentice-Hall, 1974.

Fogelin, R. J., *Understanding Arguments: An Introduction to Informal Logic.* New York: Harcourt, Brace Jovanovich, 1978.

Huff, D. *How to Lie with Statistics.* New York: W. W. Norton, 1954.

Radner, D., and M. Radner, *Science and Unreason.* Belmont, Calif.: Wadsworth, 1982.

Scriven, M. *Reasoning.* New York: McGraw-Hill, 1976.

Toulmin, S., R. Rieke, and A. Janik, *An Introduction to Reasoning.* New York: Macmillan, 1979.

Whimbey, A., and R. Lochhead, *Problem Solving and Comprehension.* Philadelphia: Franklin Institute Press, 1982, Chapter 4, on verbal reasoning problems and Chapters 6, 7, and 8 on analogies.

Theoretically Oriented Readings

Egan, D. E., and D. D. Grimes-Farrow, Differences in mental representations spontaneously adopted for reasoning, *Memory and Cognition, 10,* 297–307, 1982.

Hempel, C. G., *Philosophy of Natural Science.* Englewood Cliffs, N.J.: Prentice-Hall, 1966.

Kuhn, T. S., *The Structure of Scientific Revolutions.* Chicago: University of Chicago Press, 1962.

6

FROM CRITICISM TO CREATIVITY

The uncreative mind can spot wrong answers, but it takes a creative mind to spot wrong questions.

Anthony Jay[1]

In the previous chapter we emphasized the importance of examining the assumptions that underlie ideas and arguments. These assumptions affect how we select and interpret information and hence influence our conclusions. For example, we noted how politicians could derive different conclusions about workers' income levels by using different assumptions to select and interpret the statistics. Similarly, we illustrated how the use of analogies (a trial is like a chain or like a rope) invites assumptions that can have powerful effects on the conclusions that are drawn.

In our discussion of the IDEAL model in Chapter 2, we noted that the questioning of assumptions plays an important role in creativity—in the generation of ideas that are novel and useful. For example, we noted that people may implicitly assume that unpleasant situations (splattering bacon grease) are necessary parts of life and hence fail to *identify* the existence of problems that are potentially solvable. Similarly, *definitions* of problems often involve implicit assumptions that have important effects on our *exploration* of solutions. For example, we noted that the splattering bacon grease problem could be defined as, "People are susceptible to burns by grease" or "Hot grease travels a long distance," and that different definitions of problems usually result in different types of inventions. We also emphasized that certain implicit assumptions can make it impossible to reach solutions. For example, in the problem about the superpsychic who could predict the score of a game before it begins, most people assume that the prediction involves the final score (see Chapter 2).

Our major goal in this chapter is to discuss strategies for enhancing creative solutions to problems. We begin by considering in more detail the importance of basic assumptions. We then discuss strategies for making implicit assumptions explicit and for generating new assumptions and ideas.

THE IMPORTANCE OF BASIC ASSUMPTIONS

Historians often refer to "the Copernican revolution" as a milestone in the history of science. Copernicus was a careful and creative scientist who eventually solved a problem that others before him had failed to solve: how to account for the movement of the planets in the heavens. Astronomers had collected data indicating where various planets were at particular points in time (for example, during different months), but no one had been able to come up with a theory of their orbits that predicted where and how they would appear and that explained why.[2]

After years of study, Copernicus finally created a theory that nicely predicted the movements of the planets. To do so, however, he had to make a radical assumption. Prior to Copernicus, everyone had taken it for granted that the sun and the other planets revolve around the Earth, and indeed, it looks that way to the naked eye. Copernicus argued that, if one made this assumption, it would be impossible to predict with accuracy the movement of the planets. His theory began with an alternate assumption, namely, that the Earth and the other planets in our solar system revolve around the sun. This assumption was considered absurd and radical, so radical, in fact, that Copernicus was condemned by the Church.

Several lessons can be drawn from the example of Copernicus. One is that unnecessary assumptions (the sun and the other planets revolve around the Earth) can make it impossible to solve a problem. We have discussed this point before, but it is so important that it bears repetition. In addition, it is easy to overlook basic assumptions that reduce the creativity of our responses to problems we confront.

People who work with business executives have discovered an assumption that keeps many of them from exploring new avenues for training and employment. The assumption is, "I'm too old to try something new." In his book, *The Magic of Thinking Big,* David Schwartz describes a 40-year-old man, Cecil, who wanted to receive training for a better job yet felt that he was too old.[3] A common response to this type of problem is to suggest, "You are only as old as you feel," or to say something like, "But Ruth and Jim changed jobs at your age, and look at how well they are doing." The problem with such suggestions is that people frequently *feel* old because they believe they are old. Furthermore, it is easy to see Ruth and Jim as special cases whose situations differ in important ways.

Schwartz approached the problem in a way that directly challenged Cecil's basic assumptions. Schwartz first asked Cecil to define when a productive career began (about 20 was the answer) and to then define when one usually ends (Cecil answered "about 65 to 70"). Schwartz then helped Cecil realize that, at the age of 40, he hadn't even approached the halfway point of his career.

In working with college students, we have noticed an assumption that keeps many of them from taking more creative approaches to problems. Students are usually attempting to learn about new areas and hence view themselves as novices learning from experts. This assumption is accurate, but it is also commonplace for students to assume that, "The expert knows everything I know plus more." This latter assumption is false. Each of us has had experiences that are unique and that can help us define problems in new and interesting ways.

Consider a student we shall call Judy. Judy was writing a paper on humor and came to one of us for consultation. After talking with her it became clear that her definition of her task was to describe what "the experts" on humor had to say. Her focus was on "what they say" rather than on "what I want to know."

Further discussion with Judy revealed that she was a nursing major who had a considerable amount of experience in that area. We therefore asked how the study of humor might help people in the medical field. This led Judy to consider such statements as, "Laughter is the best medicine," and to begin to think about the degree to which humor is beneficial to sick people, and why. This approach to the problem enabled Judy to use her own knowledge about illness and hospital settings; she therefore had some criteria for evaluating the adequacy of the theories proposed by "the experts" for solving *her* problem. Needless to say, her paper turned out to be much more interesting (both to her and to us) than it would have been had she simply gone through the motions of comparing theories A, B, and C.

MAKING IMPLICIT ASSUMPTIONS EXPLICIT

The goal of identifying implicit assumptions that may be limiting our thinking is easier to describe than to achieve. Happily, there are strategies that can facilitate the discovery of alternatives. The first step is to recognize the need to consider alternatives by identifying problems with our current approach.

Searching for Inconsistencies

Our earlier discussion of Copernicus illustrates a general strategy that can prompt an examination of basic assumptions—the strategy of searching for inconsistencies. Copernicus wanted to create a theory that made precise predictions about the movements of the planets, but his initial attempts resulted in theories that were inconsistent with the actual data. His continual failure to formulate a successful theory eventually served as a signal that some of his assumptions must be erroneous. Had Copernicus not cared about the creation of a precise theory consistent with all the details of the data, the need to question basic assumptions would probably never have occurred to him.

You do not have to be a scientist to search for inconsistencies that can signal the need to examine basic assumptions. For example, after generating a possible idea or suggestion, an effective strategy is to search for alternatives that are reasonable yet contradict or are inconsistent with the idea you are considering. Consider the proverb, "He who hesitates is lost." This is undoubtedly good advice, but so is, "Haste makes waste." Additional examples of proverbs that often seem contradictory are

Nothing ventured, nothing gained.
versus
Better safe than sorry.

Absence makes the heart grow fonder.
versus
Out of sight, out of mind.

Many hands make light work.
versus
Too many cooks spoil the broth.

It seems clear that each of the proverbs provides advice appropriate *in some contexts*. When these proverbs are seen in opposition to one another, we are prompted to analyze our implicit assumptions about the contexts in which they are true. For example, the proverb, "Many hands make light work," seems to be appropriate when there is a task to be done (such as beautifying someone's yard) that can be divided into relatively independent subcomponents (raking the dead leaves, mowing the grass, and trimming around the bushes and fence). In contrast, "Too many cooks spoil the broth," is appropriate when several people are given responsibility for the same task (baking a cake) and each approaches it in a different way. Whenever someone suggests a surefire principle or strategy ("Always use mnenomic techniques to remember"), it can be beneficial to look for contradictory advice and then try to analyze the contexts within which each is true.

The strategy of searching for inconsistencies is also used by efficient technicians, doctors, and others when they are trying to evaluate the adequacy of their diagnoses of a problem. For example, a particular problem (a dead battery) usually has an associated set of symptoms (the engine won't start or turns over slowly or the lights may be dim). If the observed facts are not consistent with these symptoms (if the lights are very bright despite the fact that the motor won't start) then there is reason to doubt or reject the assumption that the problem is a dead battery. Many people often fail to evaluate the adequacy of their assumptions because they do not notice they are inconsistent with observed facts. For example, in the next paragraph the implicit assumption made by the person is inconsistent with certain facts. See if you can identify those facts.

I left work at 4:30 P.M. on Friday and got caught in the usual rush-hour traffic. When I arrived home I decided to take a shower before preparing for my trip that weekend. After packing my clothes and putting food out for the cat I decided to make a sandwich. To my horror the refrigerator was not working. Since I would be gone all weekend it was important to get it fixed before leaving early next morning. I immediately looked in the phone book and called the only refrigerator repair service. Unfortunately, no one answered the phone. This was very aggravating since the advertisement said they were open until 5 P.M.. Monday through Friday and the clock on my microwave oven showed it to be 20 minutes before five o'clock. In desperation, I went out and bought a new refrigerator at the all-night department store.

Did you notice any facts that appeared to be inconsistent with the idea that the problem was specific to the refrigerator? That the clock in the kitchen showed it to be only 4:40, which is only 10 minutes from the time the person left work (and took a shower, packed, and fed the cat), could indicate that the electrical power in the kitchen was not operating properly. To further evaluate the assumption that the problem was localized in the refrigerator it would have been helpful to check other appliances in the kitchen and check the circuit-breaker panel to see if there was another reason the refrigerator was not working. By searching for inconsistencies between what we observe and what we assume to be true, we can discover and evaluate inadequate assumptions that limit our ability to creatively respond to novel problems.

Worst-Case Analysis

Another strategy that can be important for uncovering implicit assumptions involves a worst-case analysis. The value of this strategy can be illustrated by considering the problem below.

> Imagine that you are hired as a consultant for a company that manufactures bricks. The country is in a recession, and the brick company is losing money. Your job is to save the company from financial ruin. After conducting some research you discover that the company is capable of making twice as many bricks with very little increase in operating costs. Given this, what strategies do you suggest?

Most people who have considered this problem conclude that the company should indeed make more bricks. When reminded that the company also needs to sell them, frequent responses are that more salespersons should be hired or that a new advertising campaign should be begun. These responses are quite reasonable, but they also involve some basic assumptions. The most important assumption is that there is a potential market for the bricks. Since the problem states the country is in a recession, it is a good bet the market is poor because few new houses and buildings are being built. An increase in salesmen and advertising will not solve such a problem.

Once one thinks about the problem of a market for bricks, it becomes obvious that the assumption a large market exists is questionable. Nevertheless, it would be easy to overlook this assumption and to go ahead with plans to increase brick production, advertising, and so forth (this involves *acting* on one's strategies). Once this plan fails (once one has *looked* at the effects), it is likely that the erroneous assumption will be identified. Ideally, however, we want to be able to avoid such failures by thinking things through in a way that makes erroneous assumptions clear.

As noted above, one technique for spotting erroneous assumptions involves a *worst-case analysis*. After formulating a potential solution to a problem, you simply imagine that the worst happens for each step. Given the preceding problem, for example, you might first imagine that an increase in the number of bricks manufactured increases production costs drastically rather than only slightly. This prompts a reanalysis of your assumption and hence increases the probability of detecting an error. Assume the assumption of only slight increases in costs still checks out. You might then imagine that, in the worse case, the bricks cannot be sold. This should prompt an analysis of whether a market exists.

Note that the preceding discussion of "a market" for the bricks also makes an important assumption; namely, the market is for conventional uses of bricks. If your worst-case analysis reveals a conventional market does not exist, this should provide a signal to think about alternative markets. One solution is to think of new uses for bricks to create new markets. For example, bricks might be used to make bookends, doorstops, and paperweights.

Making Predictions

Many times we are unaware or unwilling to admit we are accepting certain assumptions. These assumptions may implicitly guide our behavior and thoughts without our awareness. For instance, a male business executive who is unaware of his implicit belief that women cannot be effective managers may be biased to hire only male managers. One strategy that psychologists have used to uncover such biases or assumptions involves the practice of getting people to make predictions. Thus, we could ask the business executive to predict the success of two job applicants by looking at resumes that were identical in every way except sex. Predictions like these could be used to uncover other implicit assumptions that may bias jurors, patients, voters, and others.

The strategy of making predictions can also be used to help us probe fundamental assumptions we make in other areas. For example, to probe people's understanding of certain fundamental laws of physics, researchers have asked students to predict the direction a ball will travel when it emerges from tubes like those pictured in Figure 6.1.[4] The answers students sometimes give illustrate some

Figure 6.1
A hollow tube into which a steel ball can be dropped (resting on a flat level surface).

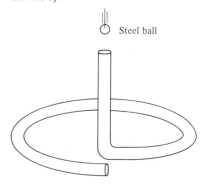

Steel ball

common misconceptions or faulty assumptions about the laws of physics. Several of these are shown in Figure 6.2. In reality, the ball would travel in a straight line approximately perpendicular to the opening.

Scientists often explore the adequacy of their theoretical assumptions by performing "thought experiments" that involve predictions. A clear example of how such thought experiments can be used to explore and evaluate assumptions was provided by Albert Einstein.[5] Einstein imagined a person riding on a streetcar that was headed away from a large clock. He then tried to predict how the clock would appear to the traveler if the car were to travel at the speed of light. He reasoned that, since the light reflecting off the clock was traveling at the same speed as the observer, the observer would always see the same image of the clock and therefore time or the clock would appear to have stopped. The results of the thought experiment helped Einstein understand the inadequacy of implicit assumptions that time is an absolute; he formulated a new relativistic concept of time. To further explore the use of predictions and thought experiments, try to imagine what the observer would see if the street car were traveling *faster* than the speed of light. (The answer appears in Appendix F.)

Seeking Criticism

A fourth strategy that can help us spot erroneous assumptions is to ask others to critique our ideas. This strategy is so obvious it may seem silly to mention it at all. Nevertheless, many people fail to seek criticism because they do not like to receive it. Others ask for criticism and then get defensive when people actually provide some. It takes some courage to seek and use criticism. Nevertheless, it is important to use this strategy because it is one of the most powerful.

GENERATING NEW IDEAS

Our preceding discussion emphasized strategies for recognizing the need to examine basic assumptions. These strategies are extremely important because

Figure 6.2
Some predicted paths of motion.

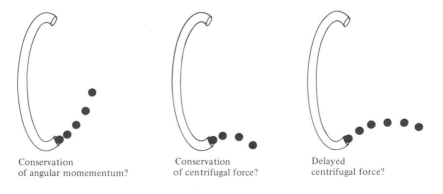

Conservation
of angular momementum?

Conservation
of centrifugal force?

Delayed
centrifugal force?

they can enable us to avoid serious problems in the future. Nevertheless, knowledge of the *need* to generate alternatives does not guarantee appropriate alternatives will in fact be found.

Analyzing Components

A number of strategies can increase the probability of generating novel alternatives. One is related to what de Bono, author of *Lateral Thinking,* calls *fractionation*.[6] The goal is to break ideas into component parts and thereby free oneself from various limiting assumptions. The term "functional fixedness" is often used to describe people's tendency to think about objects only with respect to their most characteristic function.[7] The strategy of fractionation is designed to help people notice functions and properties not typically associated with objects. For example, consider once again the problem of generating ideas for possible uses of bricks. Rather than focus only on bricks per se, it is helpful to fractionate bricks into more basic properties and consider uses for each one. Thus, a brick is red, has weight, is rectangular, is heavy, is porous, does not conduct electricity, is rough, is small enough to be picked up in one hand, holds heat, and so forth.

Most people find that the strategy of fractionating concepts (their concept of a brick) into component parts increases considerably the number of potential uses they can generate. Furthermore, if people try to generate uses but do not explicitly employ the strategy of first thinking about individual properties of concepts, their responses usually reflect implicit assumptions about properties. For example, a person who generates "doorstop," "paperweight," and "bookend" as uses of bricks is probably thinking about the property of weight even though he or she may not realize it. As noted earlier, by making our assumptions explicit we increase our opportunities to break away from them and hence become able to approach problems from new points of view.

Here is another problem.

Consider ways to reduce the sound from highways.

An analysis of this problem into components can also help you generate ideas. For example, you might first think of the major entities involved in the problem; that is, roads, cars and trucks, people (who presumably are the ones bothered by noise), and some medium (such as air) that carries sound. You could then think about the individual properties of each of these entities. For example, people have ears that might be covered to reduce the perception of noise, cars and trucks have tires that might affect noise, and so forth. Such activities can facilitate creative thought.[8]

The Use of Analogies

The use of analogies also seems to facilitate creative thinking. For example, the psychologist John Hayes describes a meeting on the problem of campus housing.[9] Someone suggested, "We have BYOB (bring your own booze) parties; why not a

BYOH (bring your own housing) university?" Hayes notes that, although this idea was suggested partly as a joke, it was in fact quite beneficial; it opened up a discussion of ways to use mobile housing units. Prior to this time, discussion had focused only on conventional housing, such as dorms—housing that is expensive to build and impossible to move around.

Analogies have also played a key role in the evolution of science and technology. For example, Benjamin Franklin noticed that a pointed object would draw a much stronger spark than a blunt object when both were in the vicinity of an electrified body.[10] However, he originally thought this was an unimportant observation. Until he recognized the analogy between clouds and electrified bodies he did not realize that pointed rods of iron could be used to protect buildings and ships from damage by lightning. Similarly, Gutenberg's invention of the printing press was developed in part from the analogies he saw in the wine press and the punches used for making coins. Another illustration of the key role analogies can play in facilitating great discoveries was provided in the reflections of August Wilhelm Kekulé 25 years after he published his model for the structure of the benzene molecule.[11]

> I turned my chair to the fire and dozed, he relates. Again the atoms were gambolling before my eyes. This time the smaller groups kept modestly in the background. My mental eye, rendered more acute by repeated visions of this kind, could now distinguish larger structures, of manifold conformation; long rows, sometimes more closely fitted together; all twining and twisting in snakelike motion. But look! What was that? One of the snakes had seized hold of its own tail, and the form whirled mockingly before my eyes.

Using the analogy of a snake biting its own tail, Kekulé was able to develop a model for the ringlike structure of the benzene molecule that profoundly affected the science of organic chemistry.

In addition to facilitating the discovery of new facts and the creation of new inventions, analogies also provide alternative frameworks for interpreting familiar facts. For example, in a recent period of stock-market decline, one analyst criticized the gloomy predictions of most of his colleagues and argued instead that the market would experience a substantial gain. His reasoning was based on an analogy to a diving board—the more downward pressure put on a diving board, the greater the tendency for it to push upward. We question the appropriateness of this analogy, but the market *did* experience a bullish period shortly thereafter. Even imperfect analogies may sometimes be useful if they lead to creative solutions. The effect of analogic thinking on creativity was perhaps best expressed by William J. Gordon when he said that analogies make the strange familiar and the familiar strange.[12]

Brainstorming

Note that such strategies as fractionation and the use of analogies can be employed in groups as well as individually. However, certain procedures must be followed in groups. For example, imagine a group setting where the common response to a new idea is to immediately say, "That sounds ridiculous," or, "I can't see any value in that suggestion." Most people will become very cautious in such situations.

In 1957, Osborn described the concept of *brainstorming*.[13] His goal was to use a group setting to increase the production of creative ideas. One of the most important characteristics of a brainstorming session is that participants must adopt an attitude of complete friendliness and an openness to suggestions. Initially, wild ideas are encouraged, the wilder the better. Furthermore, members of a brainstorming group must agree to withhold the evaluation of ideas until later in the session; hence, criticism is ruled out. This latter rule is extremely important. Since novel ideas often differ from conventional wisdom, premature evaluations can keep one from appreciating their value.

Incubation

In the preceding discussion we assumed that you continue to work on a problem until you solve it. However, if you have ever worked on a difficult problem for some length of time, on ideas for a speech or paper, for example, you have probably found that, at some point, you had to stop thinking about the problem for a while. This is not merely because of mental fatigue—it is frequently possible to think about other issues. For many people, the reason for stopping is that they find themselves coming up with the same old answers. They are locked into a particular way of thinking and need to break out.

The term "incubation" refers to the period of time when one has stopped working on a problem for a while. For example, some people think about a problem before going to bed in the hope that ideas will "incubate" (hatch) during the night and fresh insights will be available when they wake up. And indeed, this sometimes seems to occur. Many scientists have written about situations in which "flashes of insight" occurred to them after they had stopped thinking about a problem and done something else (took a trip, read a novel, or slept).[14] The following quotation is from the French mathematician Henri Poincaré.[15]

> One evening contrary to my custom, I drank black coffee and could not sleep. Ideas rose in crowds; I felt them collide until pairs interlocked, so to speak, making a stable combination. By the next morning, I had established the existence of a class of Fuchsian functions, those which come from the hypergeometric series; I had only to write out the results, which took but a few hours.

Note that, in Poincaré's case, there was a great deal of preparation before he reached any insight; he had spent a large amount of time working on his problem. The same is true for other scientists who have reported the role of insight in their work. The entire insight process has been characterized as involving four phases: (1) preparation phase, when you work hard on a problem and understand it; (2) incubation phase, when you stop working on the problem; (3) illumination phase, when a new insight occurs; and (4) elaboration phase, when the implications of the insight are worked out.

An important question is, "What happens during incubation?" An answer to this question could have important implications. For example, it could help us understand whether we should never think about the problem during incubation, whether sleep is better than any other activity, and so forth.

One possibility of the processes that occur during incubation is that the "unconscious mind" works on the problem. A weakness of this view is that we don't know what the unconscious mind is or does. Nevertheless, if you believe that the unconscious does its best work when not interfered with by the conscious mind, then the best procedure during incubation is probably to avoid thinking about the problem you want to solve, perhaps by going to sleep.

Another view of the benefits of incubation is that, with time, we cease making implicit assumptions that were preventing an adequate solution. Land, the inventor of the Polaroid Land Camera, once described insight as "the sudden cessation of stupidity."[16] This is consistent with the view that incubation may help us stop making inappropriate assumptions. Like the unconscious process theory, this view of insight also seems to suggest we should not think about the problem during the incubation phase. During the preparation phase of problem solving, however, it suggests we might try to make our current assumptions as explicit as possible to increase the likelihood that alternatives might emerge.

Still another view of the incubation phase is that it provides the opportunity to process new information that serves as a clue for solution. If problem solvers are focused only on the problem to be solved they might miss information that could serve as potential clues. However, if they keep the problem "in the back of their minds" while doing other things they may increase the probability of finding effective clues.

Consider the following list of words and phrases.

cowbell
parachute
trumpet
roof
tree

These probably don't suggest anything special; for example, they probably don't produce an insight or feeling of "aha."

Assume now that you have been trying to solve the problem of comprehending the following statement: "The haystack was important because the cloth ripped." Assume further that after working on it for a while you stop and do other things, one of which is to read the list presented above. This time parts of the list (parachute) may provide a clue for problem solution.[17] If you had kept working on the problem you probably would not have read the list. Furthermore, if the problem had not been in the back of your mind, the insight value of "parachute" would not have occurred to you.

Darwin notes that, while trying to develop a theory that could account for the data he had collected regarding similarities and dissimilarities among different species, he happened to read an essay by Thomas Malthus on population.[18] According to Darwin, the essay helped him formulate the theory of evolution despite the fact that it was about a different topic. Had Darwin simply sat in a room pondering his data he may very well not have read Malthus's article. And if Darwin had not had the general problem of accounting for his data in "the back of his mind," it seems clear that Malthus's work would not have had the clue value it did.

Note that this perspective on incubation suggests we can take an active role rather than merely sleep or avoid thinking about a problem. Thus, we can talk with others, read books, look at magazines, view scenery, and so forth. If we keep our problem in the back of our minds, we may find a host of clues that facilitate our problem-solving task.

Attempts to Communicate

Another strategy for developing creative ideas is to attempt to communicate your ideas as clearly as possible, preferably in writing, since written language persists over time and hence can be subjected to more intense evaluation. Note that attempts to express ideas in a form others will readily understand is often thought to be a process distinct from the creation of the ideas. That people should think this is probably a reflection of the way society and educational institutions have typically viewed the subjects of writing and communication. Writing and communication skills are usually taught independently of such content areas as physics, psychology, and mathematics. However, if we ask experienced writers, speakers, and researchers how they develop their ideas we usually find that the development of ideas occurs to a great degree during the process of trying to put those ideas into a communicable form. That this should be the case is entirely consistent with the IDEAL model. *Acting* on ideas by putting them in a communicable form allows us to *look* back at them and evaluate their merits. We can then use that evaluation to help us more clearly identify and define our ideas.

Most experienced writers find that they make many passes through a process similar to the IDEAL cycle before they have completed a manuscript. In fact, one difference between experienced writers and novices is the importance each assigns to the process of rewriting. The experienced writer sees writing as a technique for learning and discovery, whereas the novice tends to view it as a chore analogous to "tidying up" (fixing sentence structure and words).

Here is a simple example of discovery that can take place during writing. When we were first planning this book we knew we wanted to have a section on the use of analogies. Because of the implicit assumption that all uses of analogy were similar, we thought that one section on analogies would be all we would need. As we began writing various chapters, however, it became clear that there were some very different ways analogies could be used. For example, they are often used (1) as a basis for arguments (see Chapter 5). Earlier in this chapter, we also argued that analogies can be used (2) to facilitate the generation of new ideas, and in the next chapter we discuss how they can (3) help the communication of ideas. In retrospect, these different uses of analogies now seem obvious to us, but they were not obvious earlier. Writing and other attempts to communicate (such as attempts to teach) can therefore function as discovery techniques.

SUMMARY

In this chapter we explored how the IDEAL approach to problem solving can enhance creativity. Unlike many popular accounts of creativity, which seem to suggest that novel ideas simply "come from nowhere," we emphasized the importance of identifying and defining the basic assumptions that underlie our approach to particular problems ("I'm too old to retrain for a new job," or, "These experts know everything I know plus more"). These assumptions often keep us from approaching problems in more creative ways.

It would be nice if we could simply ask ourselves about the basic assumptions we are making and have this information immediately available to us. Unfortunately, we generally cannot do this; many of our assumptions are implicit and hence are not directly available to the consciousness. Nevertheless, there are strategies we can use to help make implicit assumptions explicit. We discussed such strategies as looking for inconsistencies, making predictions, analyzing the worst case, and seeking criticism from others. These strategies do not guarantee we will uncover all our implicit assumptions, but they certainly help.

We also emphasized that the recognition of assumptions ("We have been considering only conventional uses for our bricks") provides no guarantee one will be able to generate a wide range of possible alternatives. We therefore discussed a number of strategies that can increase the generation of novel ideas. These included the analysis of problems into components (thinking about different properties of bricks), the use of analogies, brainstorming, incubation, and active attempts to communicate. When used appropriately, these strategies can help us approach problems in much more creative ways.

EXERCISES

1. Generate some inventions (ones that you make up as well as ones that you already know about) that can help people appreciate the sights and sounds of tropical fish while remaining in their homes (one invention would be an aquarium). Generate as many as you can within 3 minutes.
2. Two men played checkers. They played five games, and each man won three. How is this possible?
3. Six normal drinking glasses are standing in a row. The first three are full of water; the next three are empty. By handling and moving only one glass, change the arrangement so that no full glass is next to another full glass, and no empty glass is next to another empty one.
4. Generate as many reasons as you can why, when my cousin comes to visit me in my apartment, he always gets off the elevator five floors below my floor and walks the rest of the way.

5. How could you make a tennis ball go a short distance, come to a dead stop, then reverse itself and go in the opposite direction? *Note*: Bouncing the ball is not permitted, nor can you put spin on the ball and roll it (this is really a form of bouncing it) or tie anything to the ball.

6. Add one line to IX to make six.

7. Look at the nine dots drawn below. The problem is to connect all of them by using only four straight lines and never retracing a line or removing your pen or pencil from the table as you draw.

8. Try solving this mystery.

A county sheriff arrived at the scene of an apparent homicide and found the victim lying on the side of the road, dead. The only clue to the crime was a pair of tire tracks left on the little-traveled dirt road. The sheriff followed the tracks to a country farmhouse less than a mile away. Although there were three men sitting on the front porch, the sheriff was certain that the man he wanted for questioning was sitting in the middle even though he knew that none of the men had a car and none had mud on their boots. How did the sheriff know he should question the man sitting in the middle?

9. Do you see any inconsistencies in the passage below? If so, are there ways they might be resolved?

The man was worried. His car came to a halt, and he was all alone. It was extremely dark and cold. The man took off his overcoat, rolled down the window, and got out of the car as quickly as possible. Then he used all his strength to move as fast as he could. He was relieved when he finally saw the lights of the city, even though they were far away.

NOTES

[1]J. Antony, *Management and Machiavelli; An Inquiry into the Politics of Corporate Life*. New York: Holt, Rinehart & Winston, 1967.

[2]One of Copernicus's important predictions about *how* planets should appear was that Venus and Mercury should go through phases like the moon does. See, for example, C. Sagan, *Broca's Brain*. New York: Ballantine, 1980.

[3]D. Schwartz, *The Magic of Thinking Big*. New York: Cornerstone Library, 1981.

[4]B. F. Green, M. McCloskey, and A. Caramazza, The relation of knowledge to problem solving, with examples from kinematics. In S. Chipman, J. Segal, and R. Glaser (Eds.), *Thinking and Learning Skills: Relating Instruction to Basic Research*, Vol. 2. Hillsdale, N.J.: Erlbaum, in press.

[5]Einstein's thought experiments. Also see T. Kuhn, A function for thought experiments. In P. N. Johnson-Laird and P. C. Wason (Eds.), *Thinking; Readings in Cognitive Science*. Cambridge, England: Cambridge Univ. Press, 1977.

[6]E. de Bono, *Lateral Thinking*. New York: Harper & Row, 1970.

[7]Experiments demonstrating "functional fixedness" were conducted by K. Dunker, On problem solving, *Psychological Monographs, 58*(5), No. 270, 1945.

[8]The use of checklists of "idea spurring thoughts" can also enhance creativity. For example, see A. F. Osborn, *Applied Imagination* (3rd revised Ed.). New York: Scribner's, 1963.

[9]J. R. Hayes, *Cognitive Psychology: Thinking and Creating*. Homewood, Ill.: Dorsey, 1978.

[10]See A. Koestler, *The Act of Creation*. New York: Macmillan, 1964.

[11]See Koestler, 1964 (note 10).

[12]W. J. Gordon, *Synectics: The Development of Creative Capacity*. New York: Harper & Row, 1961.

[13]A. Osborn, *Applied Imagination*. New York: Scribner's, 1957.

[14]See D. N. Perkins, *The Mind's Best Work*. Cambridge, Mass.: Harvard University Press, 1981.

[15]H. Poincaré, Mathematical creation. In *The Foundations of Science* (G. H. Halstead, Trans.). New York: Science Press, 1913.

[16]This example is from G. I. Nierenberg, *The Art of Creative Thinking*. New York: Simon & Schuster, 1982.

[17]This analysis of insight is from J. D. Bransford and K. E. Nitsch, Coming to understand things we could not previously understand. In J. F. Kavanagh and W. Strange (Eds.), *Speech and Language in the Laboratory, School and Clinic*. Cambridge, Mass.: MIT Press, 1978.

[18]This example is discussed in more detail in Perkins, 1981 (note 14).

SUGGESTED READINGS

Practically Oriented Readings

Adams, J. L., *Conceptual Blockbusting* (2nd Ed.). New York: W. W. Norton, 1979.

Anderson, B. F., *The Complete Thinker*. Englewood Cliffs, N.J.: Prentice-Hall, 1980, Chapter 4 on creative thinking.

Anderson, H. H. (Ed.), *Creativity and Its Cultivation*. New York: Harper & Row, 1959.

de Bono, E., *Lateral Thinking*. New York: Harper & Row, 1970.

Gordon, W. J., *Synectics: The Development of Creative Capacity*. New York: Harper & Row, 1961.

Osborn, A. F., *Applied Imagination: Principles and Procedures of Creative Problem Solving* (3rd revised Ed.). New York: Scribner's, 1963.

Theoretically Oriented Readings

Bradshaw, G. F., P. W. Langley, and H. Simon, Studying scientific discovery by computer simulation, *Science, 222,* 971–975, 1983.

Koestler, A., *The Act of Creation*. New York: Macmillan, 1964.

Kuhn, T. S., *The Structure of Scientific Revolutions*. Chicago: University of Chicago Press, 1962.

Stein, M. I., *Stimulating Creativity*. New York: Academic Press, 1974.

Watzlawick, P., J. H. Weakland, and R. Fisch, *Change: Principles of Problem Formation and Problem Resolution*. New York: W. W. Norton, 1974.

7

EFFECTIVE COMMUNICATION

What is there greater than the word which persuades the judges in the courts, or the senators in the council, or the citizens in the assembly, or at any other political meeting?

(Plato, *Dialogues*)[1]

In the preceding chapter we emphasized the importance of making implicit assumptions explicit, and we discussed strategies for generating new ideas. These new ideas must be communicated to others for them to have an important impact; the failure to communicate what you consider to be a good idea can be extremely frustrating.

Effective speakers and authors use a variety of strategies to facilitate communication. For example, they select strategies as a function of *with whom* they are attempting to communicate, *how* they are attempting to communicate (orally or in writing), and *what* they are attempting to accomplish. The major goal of this chapter is to discuss how different strategies are appropriate depending upon the communication problems you face.

THE NATURE OF THE AUDIENCE

One of the most important requirements for defining the nature of communication problems is to learn about your audience. Different communication strategies are necessary depending on the knowledge, interests, attitudes, and customs of the people you plan to address. As an obvious example, it would not be wise to speak English to a group of people who understood only French. Even when people can speak your language, however, you must communicate differently depending on what they already know. For example, if you wanted to help third and fourth graders learn something about problem solving you could probably find a way to do so, but it is doubtful you would use the strategy of suggesting they read this book. Most children in the third and fourth grades can read, but they do not have enough background knowledge to understand many of the concepts and examples used in this book.[2]

Here is a message that can communicate meaningful information under some conditions. Try to figure out a situation in which this message would make sense.[3]

If the balloons popped, the sound would not be able to carry since everything would be too far away from the correct floor. A closed window would also prevent the sound from carrying since most buildings tend to be well insulated. Since the whole operation depends on a steady flow of electricity, a break in the middle of the wire would also cause problems. Of course the fellow could shout, but the human voice is not loud enough to carry that far. An additional problem is that a string could break on the instrument. Then there could be no accompaniment to the message. It is clear that the best situation would involve less distance. Then there would be fewer potential problems. With face-to-face contact, the least number of things could go wrong.

Most people have a difficult time understanding this message. Given the information illustrated in Figure 7.1, however, the message makes sense (look at the picture and then read the passage again). This message would be quite comprehensible if you delivered it to an audience that already possessed the relevant background information. However, for people who did not possess this information, the same message would not make sense.

We frequently need to discuss particular topics despite the fact that many members of our audience do not possess extensive background knowledge in that area. If you are a lawyer, for example, you may need to communicate information about biology, psychiatry, or physics to the members of a jury. The use of metaphors, analogies, and concrete examples can be very helpful in these types of situations. Consider Nigel Calder's use of metaphor and analogy to communicate information about a black hole in space. He refers to it as "a great starswallower. . . . When stars or gas [come] close to it they [swirl] in faster and faster like water approaching a plug hole."[4] This is a very helpful analogy *provided* that people have already acquired some knowledge of what it is like for water to swirl down a drain or plughole. To evaluate the appropriateness of analogies and examples, you must know something about your audience's knowledge base.

Factual information may also need to be presented in different ways depending on your audience. For example, imagine you want to communicate, "By the time they graduate from high school, American children have watched an average of 18,000 hours of television." Whether members of your audience understand the significance of this depends on the degree to which they are used to thinking in such units as thousands of hours. For most people you will need to supply information that can make such facts more meaningful. For example, you might help them see that this figure amounts to several hours of TV viewing each day, or you might note that 18,000 hours is more time than most of these students have spent in school. The types of units and comparisons that are most meaningful will depend on what your audience already knows.

Communication across Cultures

The task of creating messages appropriate for our audience can be especially difficult when we try to communicate with members of different cultures or subcultures. Since most of us tend to take our cultural knowledge for granted, we frequently fail to realize that others may not share our view of the world. For example, researchers have presented Americans and natives of India with written descriptions of (1) an American wedding and (2) an Indian wedding.[5] Although members of both groups knew something about weddings, they frequently misinterpreted aspects of the other culture's ceremony. For example, the description of the American wedding included information that the bride wore "something old, something new, something borrowed, and something blue." The Americans realized this was part of a tradition, but many of the Indians interpreted it differently. They felt sorry for the bride because she had to borrow things and had to wear clothes that were old.

The Indians' misinterpretations of the American wedding (and vice versa) are unlikely to have serious international ramifications. Nevertheless, it is easy to imagine other situations in which differences in interpretations can have unfortunate consequences. For example, in America, the statement, "When the going gets tough, the tough get going," is usually interpreted as an emphasis on the importance of self-determination. When uttered to members of another culture, however, it could be seen as an attempt to bully by reference to a threat of war.

Cross-cultural communication is often a problem for companies doing business in foreign lands. For example, an article in *The Wall Street Journal* described an incident in which a United States firm asked its Japanese distributor to advertise a new product.[6] The Japanese distributor answered in the affirmative. A year later the owner of the United States firm found that not a single advertisement had been placed. He later realized that saying yes in Japan does not necessary mean, "Yes, I will do it." Instead, it often means, "Yes, I understand."

Many attempts to communicate involve nonverbal as well as verbal messages. Like verbal messages, nonverbal messages can also be misinterpreted across cultures. For instance, patterns of eye contact can have different implications for communication. In America, it is generally considered important to "look people in the eye." If, when meeting an American, you glance at his or her eyes and then quickly look elsewhere, you will frequently be perceived as unsure of yourself or perhaps rude. In other cultures, however, direct eye contact can have other meanings. For example, in some American Indian tribes young children are taught that it is disrespectful to look an elder in the eye. Non-Indians who value eye contact can therefore seem disrespectful to Indians. Analogously, American Indian children are often perceived by white teachers as disinterested because the children look away from the teachers rather than look them in the eye.[7]

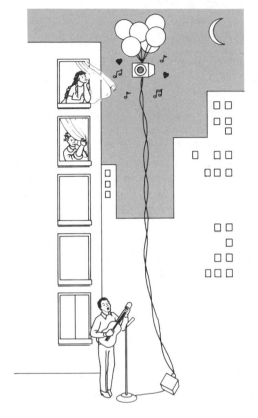

Figure 7.1
A picture that allows people to understand the passage about the balloons.

MODES OF COMMUNICATION

The strategies necessary for effective communication also depend on the manner in which we try to communicate. For example, we may converse with someone face to face, talk on television where people can see us but cannot interact, talk on radio where we can be heard but not seen, or "talk" by means of writing where we can neither be seen nor heard. The most basic differences in modes of communication are those that separate speaking and writing.[8] These two modes require the use of different strategies, and they each have advantages and disadvantages of their own.

Some Advantages of Speaking

Given the choice of holding a friendly face-to-face conversation versus writing a letter or paper, most people prefer the conversation. One reason is that oral communication is faster than written communication—most people speak much faster than they write. The slowness of writing is one of the major reasons people often say they do not like writing. They feel its slowness interferes with their thinking, which frequently seems quite fast.

Another advantage of speaking over writing is that speakers can utilize a greater variety of information. For example, they can use facial expressions, gestures, and different types of intonation to make their messages clear. In addition, speakers usually have a number of chances to clarify their intended meanings because the people with whom they are talking can ask questions or indicate they do not understand. In contrast, writers are usually isolated from their audience, and they are unable to rely on extra sources of information, such as the immediate nonverbal context or gestures. Writers must therefore work hard to state their ideas with clarity and to avoid ambiguity. Many people do not like this extra work.

Some Advantages of Writing

Although writing *does* need to be less ambiguous than spoken language and *is,* slower, it is important to note that it also has its advantages. An extremely important one is that writing persists over time and space and hence can be analyzed with considerably more care than can spoken language. Indeed, some theorists argue that the invention of written language was one of the hallmarks of human development because it enabled people to become much more precise in their analyses of arguments.

One way to appreciate the greater precision of written language is to analyze the nature of written versus spoken sentences. If you tape-record everyday conversations and then type them word for word, you will be amazed at the number of false starts, pauses, "hm's," and other imperfections. The linguist Wallace Chafe provides the following illustrations.[9]

> I'm feeling OK now (laugh), but uh I had last week I thought I was (laugh) dying. You heard that I fainted in the shower.

When we are listening to others we tend not to notice all the false starts and pauses. When we write, however, we are expected to produce sentences that are well organized. Our statements, therefore, need to be more carefully planned and evaluated.

That written language persists over time and space also has advantages that go beyond the individual sentence level. Since information can be stored externally, it is easier to compare statements made earlier with those made later. This frequently leads to the detection of inconsistencies in arguments and hence enables the writer to rethink his or her ideas.

An additional advantage of writing over speaking is that, in writing, we do not have to begin at the beginning and proceed in order until we reach the end. *Papers can be written in any order we choose.* Interestingly, many students do not realize this at first and hence may spend hours trying to find "just the right" introductory sentence or paragraph. Experienced writers frequently skip the introduction or spend very little time on it because they realize that, as they write, they will get a better idea of their central idea or thesis and hence will end up redoing the introduction anyway. Experienced writers also realize they can work on different pieces of a paper at various times. Thus, if you know that at some point in your paper you will have to supply background information about your main charcter, you can write this at any time: at a time when you need to incubate other ideas, for example. Writing permits a great deal of flexibility with respect to the order of strategies you use.[10]

Interactive Computer Programs

Modern computer technology makes it possible to create new forms of communication that combine some of the advantages of spoken and written messages. The ability to create programs that *interact* with users (your audience) provides one illustration. Imagine you want to write a letter to somecne (your mother) but that you want to program it on a computer and store it on a disk rather than write it on paper (you therefore send the disk to your mother, who needs to have a computer that can use it). You might program the disk so that, when your mother uses it with her computer, her screen says: "Hi, Mom. I have several different kinds of things to tell you. Please choose the topic you want to start with."

Your computer program might then provide a "menu" of topics, such as (1) "How I spent my summer vacation," (2) "When I could come to visit," and (3) "Why I want to get married next month." By selecting either 1, 2, or 3, your mother could then read about each topic in the order she chooses. In addition, you could program little "tests" that increase the probability your intended message is conveyed. For example, after your mother had read part of your messge, you could provide choices that allow her to indicate her reaction. Thus, you might ask, "What do you think about what I've just told you?" Choices might be (a) "I'm elated," (b) "It's okay, but certainly not great," or (c) "You are disinherited." Your program could then respond in different ways depending on your mother's answer (depending on how she interacted with your program). If she chose, "You are disinherited," for example, your program could respond with, "Wait a minute, you must have misunderstood somthing," and so forth. The creation of interactive computer programs has the potential to provide a method of communication that permits an interaction in which answers depend on questions. In addition, the message can persist across space and time.

COMMUNICATION GOALS

We have noted that strategies for communication must vary depending on the nature of our audience and our mode of presentation. The effectiveness of different strategies also depends on our overall communication goal.

Imagine that your goal is to win an election. If your audience (your electorate) includes a variety of conflicting perspectives, you may purposely want to be ambiguous. For example, you may state, "You know what is needed and I am going to do it," in the hope that different groups of people will make invited inferences favorable to your position. We do not view the goal of ambiguity as lofty. Nevertheless, it seems to be a goal that people occasionally adopt.

In everyday social conversations the major goal is frequently to maintain social contact rather than to analyze arguments with precision. For example, imagine that your, "How are you?" is answered by, "I'm having a rough day; I can't seem to remember anything." It is unlikely that you will worry about the ambiguous use of the term "memory" and ask, "Are you talking about short-term memory or long-term memory? Do you think you have a storage deficit or a retrieval deficit?" Instead, you will probably say something like, "I know what you mean." On the other hand, imagine that you write a paper on memory and use the term "memory" ambiguously; you will almost undoubtedly be criticized. This illustrates a difference between written and spoken language that was not discussed earlier; namely the audience and goals of the two modes of communication frequently differ. For example, when students write papers they generally write to an audience (their teachers) that is much more demanding than their peers and that has different goals in mind.

The Use of Jargon

Speakers and writers often use special terms, often referred to as jargon, in order to accomplish various goals. One goal is to communicate in an efficient manner. For example, if a scientist is able to describe her study as involving "an A-B, A-C retroactive interference paradigm," this represents an extremely efficient way to communicate *provided* that members of the intended audience are familiar with the technical terms used.

Jargon can also be used for a variety of other purposes. One is to make the impact of a message less direct and hence seem less objectionable. For example, Edwin Newman, a recognized authority on the uses and abuses of the English language, notes that in today's world people are often "outplaced" rather than "fired."[11] Others are "transportation disadvantaged," which simply means they do not own a car. Another example of jargon designed to make information seem more palatable is "strategic retrograde action," a phrase used to describe retreat during the Vietnam War.

Speeches and papers often reflect the existence of multiple goals. For example, we may want to communicate yet want to appear knowledgeable as well. Students who receive assignments to write papers often use jargon because they feel the need to "appear knowledgeable." Consider the following introduction to a paper on economics.[12]

The persistent economic woes that now plague the United States will not be vanquished, or even substantially curbed, until new currents of thought emerge within the federal government that will force it to commence with the difficult policies required to assuage our present problems.

This introduction seems sophisticated at first glance, but what does it mean? Daniel Fader, a prominent writing expert, describes his interactions with the economics student who wrote this essay. Fader's first request of the student was to state what he meant by his first sentence by putting it into his own words. The student's response to Fader's question was as follows:

> "Well . . . yeah . . . America's worst economic problems won't be solved until the government . . . until the government comes up with some tough new policies."

Fader then asked why the student had not written this initially: why all the "woes" and "plague" and "vanquished" and "assuage"? The student's answer is revealing.

> That's just the kind of stuff you use to write about Economics and . . . and things like that," he replies.

It is possible that some teachers place more emphasis on the use of "sophisticated-sounding" words than on the clarity of a message, but this has not been our experience. Teachers we know, including ourselves, value papers that provide a clear and concise statement of the author's ideas. Indeed, we find that students who rely too heavily on sophisticated-sounding terms frequently are unclear about their intended message—they are really not sure what they mean.

Achieving Clarity

An excellent strategy for improving the clarity of written communication is to try to restate something you have written in your own words, and to state it in as simple a way as possible. This frequently helps people discover problems with what they have written and enables them to clarify what they really want to say. For example, consider once again the preceding introduction to the economics paper. As the student tried to paraphrase his introduction by putting it into his own words, he developed a much better understanding of the issues. He eventually began his paper by advising the government to develop tough new economic policies based on economic *facts* rather than on economic *politics*.[13] This represents a definition of a problem that seems interesting and important. Had the student not been prompted to *act* on his ideas and *look* at the effects, he probably would have failed to clarify the nature of the problem he wanted to address.

The experience of the economics student is not unusual. We have noted several times that people often begin to talk or write without having a clear idea of what they want to say. Many people find they have not really defined the basic problem they are trying to address until the end of their first or second (and sometimes even more) drafts of a paper or speech.[14] Through speaking or writing they are able to clarify their ideas. Effective problem solvers use these clarifications to structure new drafts, drafts that begin with the newly defined problem and reach an effective conclusion. Effective problem solvers also evaluate their work in terms of criteria such as those discussed below.

CRITERIA FOR EVALUATING THE EFFECTIVENESS OF COMMUNICATION

Many people's criterion for evaluating their speech or paper is "whatever is ready in time for the deadline." Since the ability to communicate can have such important effects on people's careers, it is desirable to have criteria that surpass that just mentioned. Different chapters in this book provide useful criteria for evaluating your work. For example, you can ask yourself whether you have tried to

1. *Help your audience understand the general problem you want to address, and show them how it can be defined from a variety of perspectives and how different problem definitions can lead to different strategies for solution.* It can also be beneficial to explain the inadequacies of various solutions, to set the stage for redefining the problem and trying a new approach (see Chapter 2).

2. *Organize your speech or talk in a way that will make the main points easy to identify and remember.* For example, you could use visual aids to illustrate main points or you could suggest helpful acronyms or acrostics. Try to ensure that whatever prompts you use are sufficient to act as effective retrieval cues later on (see Chapter 3).

3. *Include the type of background information, examples, and analogies that will enable listeners or readers to understand the significance of facts rather than be faced with sets of seemingly arbitrary facts.* Also, remember that different levels of understanding are necessary depending on people's goals. Provide just the level of precision you think your audience needs, no more and no less (see Chapter 4).

4. *Make sure that your facts and your interpretations of these facts are accurate, and check for logical fallacies and inconsistencies.* In addition, analyze the assumptions that underlie your arguments and ask yourself whether they are reasonable (Chapter 5).

5. *Include information that is novel and useful rather than merely restate things most people already know.* If some of your statements seem obvious ("Haste makes waste"), you can help people see that contradictory statements also seem obvious ("He who hesitates is lost"). By creating a tension between two "obvious" yet contradictory beliefs, you can help people see the need to focus on the contexts in which each is true (see Chapter 6).

6. *Pay careful attention to your audience and your goals, and evaluate these according to your mode of communication.* Anticipate as many possibilities for miscommunication as you can, and select your strategies accordingly. In addition, *look* at the effects of your attempts to communicate and learn from your mistakes.

SUMMARY

In this chapter we emphasized that effective communicators *identify* and *define* the particular communication problems they face and *explore* appropriate strategies.

Effective communicators also *act* on the basis of their strategies and *look* at the effects; hence, they continue to improve.

Particular emphasis was placed on the importance of defining communication problems in terms of our audience, our mode of communication, and our overall goals. For example, we noted that the intended audience has an important effect on our choice of communication strategies because audiences can vary with respect to background knowledge, interests, and customs. When we attempt to communicate with people from different cultures, all three of these factors often vary. Under these conditions, communication failures can easily occur.

We also noted that our mode of communication affects the choice of strategies. When speaking, for example, we can rely on gestures, intonation, perceptual context, and other sources of information to convey our intended meanings; these sources of information are not available when writing. Nevertheless, we emphasized that writing has advantages of its own. For example, it provides a form of external storage that makes it easier to evaluate our arguments, and it permits us to work on various subparts of a message in any order we choose. We also discussed how modern computer technology makes possible new modes of communication that combine advantages of both the oral and written modes.

Our goals as communicators also play an important role in our selection of strategies. We discussed such goals as purposely being ambiguous, communicating to maintain social contact (rather than to make precise arguments), and attempting to appear knowledgeable. We emphasized the importance of attempting to communicate with clarity and discussed strategies for achieving this goal.

Discussion also focused on criteria for evaluating a speech or paper; we noted that each chapter in this book provides an important set of criteria. For example, effective communicators help their audience define the problem to be addressed, remember the main points of the argument, and understand the significance of the information. They also make sure that their messages are free from logical fallacies and inconsistencies, and they attempt to present novel ideas and solutions rather than merely restate facts that everyone already knows.

NOTES

[1]Cited in B. Jowett, *The Dialogues of Plato*, Vol. 1. New York: Random House, 1937.

[2]See especially T. C Anderson, Role of the reader's schema in comprehension, learning and memory. In R. Anderson, J. Osborn, and R. Tierney (Eds.), *Learning to Read in American Schools: Basal Readers and Content Texts*. Hillsdale, N.J.: Erlbaum, 1984.

[3]From J. D. Bransford and M. K. Johnson, Contextual prerequisites for understanding: Some investigations of comprehension and recall, *Journal of Verbal Learning and Verbal Behavior, 11,* 717–726, 1972.

[4]N. Calder, *Einstein's Universe*. New York: Penguin, 1980.

[5]M. S. Steffensen, D. Joag-Deci, and R. C. Anderson, A cross-cultural perspective on reading comprehension, *Reading Research Quarterly, 15,* 10–29, 1979.

[6]H. Klein, Firms seek aid in deciphering Japan's culture, *The Wall Street Journal, 9–1,* 27, 1983.

[7]See R. Freedle, Interaction of language use with ethnography and cognition. In J. H.

Harvey (Ed.), *Cognition, Social Behavior and the Environment*. Hillsdale, N.J.: Erlbaum, 1981.

[8]See W. L. Chafe, Speakers and writers do different things. In P. L. Stock (Ed.), *F Forum: Essays on Theory and Practice in the Teaching of Writing*. Upper Montclair, N.J.: Boynton Cook, 1983. A. Rubin, A theoretical taxonomy of the differences between oral and written language. In R. J. Spiro, B. C. Bruce, and W. F. Brewer (Eds.), *Theoretical Issues in Reading Comprehension*. Hillsdale, N.J.: Erlbaum, 1980.

[9]From Chafe, 1983 (note 8).

[10]Excellent discussions of writing can be found in L. Flower, *Problem-Solving Strategies for Writing*. New York: Harcourt, Brace Jovanovich, 1981. S. Pearl, Understanding composing, *College and Communication, 31*, 363–369. 1980. M. Scardemalia, Written composition. In M. Witlock (Ed.), *Handbook of Research Teaching* (3rd Ed.), in press. P. L. Stock (Ed.), *F Forum: Essays on Theory and Practice in the Teaching of Writing*. Upper Montclair, N.J.: Boynton Cook, 1983.

[11] Cited in *Simply Stated: The Monthly Newsletter of the Document Design Center, American Institute for Research*, No. 32, Dec. 1982–Jan. 1983.

[12]From D. Fader, Narrowing the space between language and text. In P. L. Stock (Ed.), *F Forum: Essays on Theory and Practice in the Teaching of Writing*. Upper Montclair, N.J.: Boynton Cook, 1983.

[13]From D. Fader (note 11).

[14]See N. Sommers, Revision strategies of student writers and experienced adult writers, *College Composition and Communication, 31*, 378–388, 1980.

SUGGESTED READINGS

Practically Oriented Readings

Flower, L., *Problem-Solving Strategies for Writing*. New York: Harcourt, Brace Jovanovich, 1981.

Theoretically Oriented Readings

Freedle, R., Interaction of language use with ethnography and cognition. In J. H. Harvey (Ed.), *Cognition, Social Behavior and the Environment*. Hillsdale, N.J.: Erlbaum, 1981.

Pearl, S., Understanding composing, *Composition and Communication, 31*, 363–369, 1980.

Rubin, A., A theoretical taxonomy of the differences between oral and written language. In R. J. Spiro, B. C. Bruce, and W. F. Brewer (Eds.), *Theoretical Issues in Reading Comprehension*. Hillsdale, N.J.: Erlbaum, 1980.

Scardemalia, M., Written composition. In M. Witlock (Ed.), *Handbook of Research on Teaching* (3rd Ed.), in press.

Sommers, N., Revision strategies of student writers and experienced adult writers, *Composition and Communication, 31*, 378–388, 1980.

Steffensen, M. S., D. Joag-Deck, and R. C. Anderson, A cross-cultural perspective on reading comprehension, *Reading Research Quarterly, 15*, 10–29, 1979.

Stock, P. L. (Ed.), *F Forum: Essays on Theory and Practice in the Teaching of Writing*. Upper Montclair, N.J.: Boynton Cook, 1983.

8

CONCLUDING REMARKS

We wrote this book because of our conviction that much of what we do during our lives involves problem solving and that everyone can learn to solve problems more successfully. To accomplish this goal, it is necessary to become more aware of the variety of problems each of us faces in our everyday lives and of the processes we use in attempting to find solutions. It is for this reason we discussed the IDEAL model of problem solving and illustrated how it is applicable to a variety of domains.

Note that the goal of becoming more aware of the processes underlying problem solving does not necessarily mean you should *always* think in detail about these processes while attempting to solve problems. If you spend all your time analyzing your thinking processes you will probably find that it interferes with your ability to solve problems (try to tie your shoe or drive a car while consciously attempting to articulate each step). An awareness of the processes that underlie problem solving becomes most valuable when you are having difficulty. If you are observant, you can often catch yourself failing to (1) *identify* potential problems, (2) *define* them appropriately, (3) *explore* a variety of possible approaches, (4) *act* on your ideas, or (5) *look* at the effects of your actions. By becoming aware of these possible sources of difficulty you have a much better chance of approaching problems in optimal ways.

THE EVOLUTION OF PROBLEM-SOLVING SKILLS

One of the major themes of this book has been that the improvement of problem-solving skills is an ongoing process. By using the IDEAL model you can become more aware of the processes you use to solve problems and hence can improve your ability to notice possibilities for change. We have discussed many general strategies for improving problem-solving performance. However, we have also emphasized that one of the most powerful ways to increase your ability to solve problems is to acquire new conceptual tools. These tools can often be very specialized. For instance, if you want to solve problems involving plumbing you should learn about the tools and concepts plumbers use to simplify their tasks. Similarly, improving your ability to solve other problems may require knowledge of biology, mathematics, or finance.

Our primary goal in this book has been to discuss the kinds of activities and strategies that can help you acquire new conceptual tools. That is, as you explore new domains you will need to remember information, learn with understanding, critically evaluate ideas, formulate creative alternatives, and communicate effectively. We have discussed how the IDEAL model can be applied to each of these problems; the model should therefore help you to continue to learn on your own. At the most general level, the model focuses on the importance of understanding how the information you are trying to learn can function as tools that will enable you to solve problems more effectively.

In many formal educational settings it is frequently difficult to see how concepts and procedures can function as tools for problem solving. Students are often exposed to concepts without having a good idea of the types of problems they were designed to solve. To be a successful learner, it is important to attempt to identify and define problems relevant to the content area you are learning. An effective way to learn is therefore to become involved in the types of activities characteristic of people who work in the field you are studying; this information can provide a context for more formal types of learning, such as learning from lectures and books. For example, experiences with the types of everyday problems faced by busy business executives can provide a context for understanding and evaluating various books on management. If you know the kinds of problems faced by executives, you are in a much better position to determine whether particular books provide the kinds of conceptual tools executives need.

ATTITUDES

We noted in the first chapter of this book that one of the biggest stumbling blocks for improving problem solving can be people's negative attitudes about their abilities. It is easy to tell people to think positively about their ability to solve problems, but such suggestions often have little effect on attitudes acquired from many years of negative experiences. A lack of confidence in our ability to solve problems can manifest itself in a variety of ways; for example, it may be reflected by a lack of interest, a fear of exploring new domains, or a fear of criticism. These feelings can interefere with solving problems and can prevent us from engaging in activities that might improve our problem-solving skills. The IDEAL approach to problem solving can be especially helpful in these situations because it provides a guide for debugging unsuccessful approaches to problem solving. By identifying the attitudes that inhibit success and defining their causes we can begin to explore strategies that may overcome our earlier failures. In addition, by actively using appropriate strategies, we can build self-confidence by giving ourselves the opportunity to observe success.

The tendency to avoid new areas becomes especially strong when others are performing well while we experience considerable difficulty. A common way to define such difficulties is simply to assume we are inept or slow and others are talented. An alternate perspective is that *everyone* experiences difficulty when first learning about a new area: there is too much new information to attend to at once. If you stick with the task, however, you will find that it becomes easier and easier to perform.

As an illustration of this argument, try to remember what it was like when you were first learning to drive a car. If you are like most people, you felt extemely awkward. You probably had to explicitly think about pushing the brake, turning the wheel, using the turn signal, and so forth, and it was extremely difficult to do something like carry on a conversation while driving. With practice, however, many aspects of driving became automatic, and the task of driving and carrying on a conversation became easy to perform.

It is useful to keep the driving example in mind when you are trying to learn about new areas because your experiences will almost undoubtedly be similar. At first everything will seem so new as to be overwhelming, and people who can already perform these tasks may seem almost superhuman. Later, you will perform the tasks with little difficulty; they will become relatively automatic and require much less conscious attention. Nevertheless, to reach this stage you must be prepared to go through a period of feeling and being awkward. You must have the courage to risk making mistakes.

Research on the problem of learning a second language provides an excellent illustration of the importance of risk taking.[1] Researchers have found that an important difference between successful and less successful second language learners is that the successful students usually make a "best" guess about the meaning of an unfamiliar utterance even though they are not absolutely sure of their answer. In contrast, the less successful students often avoid taking such risks. Similarly, one of the reasons young children learn so readily seems to be that they are less self-conscious about making errors.[2] Of course, young children often do not realize that they have made an error (for example, in interpreting a statement) whereas adults are more likely to do so. Nevertheless, to be an effective problem solver we must be willing to take the chance that we may not always be correct. In short, the IDEAL problem solver realizes that problem solving is a self-correcting activity that allows for improvement *only* if we are willing to act on our best ideas.

NOTES

[1] I. Rubin, What the "good language learner" can teach us, *Teachers of English to Speakers of Other Languages Quarterly, 9,* 41–51, 1975.

[2] J. D. Bransford and K. Heldmeyer, Learning from children learning. In G. L. Bisanz and R. Kail (Eds.), *Learning in Children.* New York: Springer-Verlag, 1983.

APPENDIX A

Answer to the Bird and Train problem:
Since the two train stations are 50 miles apart and the trains are traveling toward one another, each will travel 25 miles before they meet. Both trains are traveling at the rate of 25 miles per hour, so the time it takes for them to meet is 1 hour. Since the bird flies at a rate of 100 miles per hour, it will fly 100 miles before the two trains meet.

APPENDIX B

Answer to the Boxes problem:
There are 33 boxes (3 large, 6 medium, and 24 small boxes).

Answer to the Four-Chains problem:
The most common tendency is to work only with the end links of each chain. The solution requires that you open all the links in one of the chains (for a total of 3 links open at 2 cents apiece, or 6 cents). You can then use three open links to join the remaining 3 chains together (for a total of 3 links closed at 3 cents apiece, or 9 cents).

Answer to the Trip to Chicago problem:
You need to take the 6 P.M. dinner flight, which allows you to arrive at 6 A.M. If you did not arrive until 7:30 you would be late for your meeting, since you need 20 minutes to get your luggage and 20 minutes more for a taxi ride. If you take the 6 P.M. flight you do not need to buy dinner since it is supplied on the plane.

Answer to Racquetball Tournament problem:
If you assume that only 2 people were in the tournament, you would need only one score card for that match. If 3 people entered, you would need 2 score cards (one for the first match and one for the winner of that match versus the third participant). If 4 people entered, you would need 3 cards (one for each of the two initial matches and one more when the winners of these two matches play one another). If we let N stand for the number of people who play in the tournament, the general pattern for the number of cards needed is $N - 1$.

Answer to the Cannonball problem:
There are a number of different ways to solve this problem. Here is one. On the first weighing, try 4 balls on each side. If they balance, you know that the oddball is one of the 4 not on the scale. If they do not balance, you know that the oddball is one of the 8 balls on the scale.

Assume that the balls do not balance. You can now remove 4 from one side and replace them with the 4 that were not weighed originally. Since you know this new set of 4 does not contain the oddball, you can use it as a standard for weight.

For example, assume that you weigh this "standard" against 4 balls and they balance. You now know the oddball is one of the 4 you just removed from the scale. If you also kept a record of whether these 4 balls were heavier or lighter during the second weighing, you know whether the oddball is heavier or lighter than the other balls.

Assume that you have now reduced the options to 4 balls. For your third weighing you can weigh 2 of these balls against 2 balls you know are of standard weight. If the balls balance you know that the oddball is one of only two remaining balls. You can then use your fourth weighing to balance one of these two against a standard. If they balance you know that the one remaining ball is the oddball. If they do not balance, you know that the oddball is the one not on the scale (and not the standard you have been using). This problem can also be solved using just three weighings.

Answer to the Superpsychic problem:
Before it starts, the score of any game is 0 to 0.

Answer to the Bird in the Room problem:
The instructor turned out all the lights in the seminar room so that the light from the window became very obvious. The bird immediately headed toward the light and escaped from the room (the window was still open, of course).

APPENDIX C

Answer to Credits and Debits problem:
One strategy is to think, "Credits has an R in it, so they go on the right."

Answer to Poisonous Snakes problem:
One possibility is to create a rhyme, such as, "Red and black venom lack; red and yellow kill a fellow."

Answer to Port and Starboard problem:
One strategy is to think, "Left is shorter than right, and port is shorter than starboard."

Another is to think, "Port (a type of wine) should be *left* standing before drinking it."

APPENDIX D

Assumptions Involved in Sentence Comprehension

The man was late for work because it snowed.

You probably made a number of assumptions. One is that he probably had to travel some distance to get to work. Another assumption you probably made is that it was harder than usual to get to work, presumably because of the snow.

I drove my wife to work because her bicycle had a flat tire.

You probably assumed that she lived close enough to work to ride her bicycle but not so close that she could easily walk.

The policeman held up his hand and the cars stopped.

You probably assumed that the cars had drivers who applied the brakes when they saw the policeman's signal. If the cars did not have drivers (if they were merely rolling down a hill), most people would be surprised if the cars stopped at the sight of an outstretched hand.

Answer to the Theater Joke:
The joke, which was told by Dick Cavett, is, "I have some good news and some bad news for people in the balcony. I am not going to tell you the bad news, but the good news is that the flames won't reach you for several minutes."

Answer to the Card Game problem:
If both players remove cards from the table at the same time, then neither one can run out of cards first. Furthermore, what card can be added to the card with a zero on it to add up to ten?

APPENDIX E

Answer to Typing and Grades problem:
The relationship between typed papers and higher grades is correlational. Although it is possible that students got higher grades *because* they typed their papers, it is equally possible that students who are more serious about their education were more likely to have learned to type, that students who are more motivated were more likely to take the time to type their paper, and so on.

Answer to Gas-Saving Device problem:
You would need to know whether the two cars got comparable gas mileage *before* the gas-saving device was used. In addition, you would want to be sure that the present device could be effective for other makes of cars, most importantly, the make you drive.

Answer to the Rebate problem:
You need to know how many people of each income category purchased products that had the $1 rebate form. For example, there are probably fewer people in the higher income category than in the lower and middle income categories. Furthermore, assume that only 4100 people in the higher income category purchased the product. If 4000 of them sent in for the rebate, this would be a very high percentage and could indicate that people with high incomes are *more* likely to send in rebate forms.

Answers to "If it is a triangle, then it is red" problem (If A, then B):
The first problem (if the shape is not a triangle, is it not red?) can be translated as, "If A, then B; not A, therefore not B." To reason in this manner would be to commit the fallacy of denying the antecedent. The argument is not valid.

130

The second problem (if the shape is not red, is it not a triangle?) can be translated as, "If A, then B; not B, therefore not A." This is a valid argument.

Answer to the Mop problem:
Sally used a dirty mop.

Answer to the "John is able to come to the party tonight" problem:
John was originally going to leave town in his car and hence would have had to miss the party. However, since his car broke down, he could now attend.

Answer to the Wrinkled Dress problem:
Jill does not know how to iron.

Answer to the Murder problem:
The woman cannot be prosecuted because she is a Siamese twin and the law prohibits an innocent person from being jailed.

APPENDIX F

Answer to the Einstein problem:
The clock would appear to be going backwards.

ANSWERS TO EXERCISES

Chapter 2

1. Most people produce the answer 2, which is wrong. The correct answer is 0. If you answered 2, you probably failed to identify a problem with your own understanding of the problem, namely, that it asks about Adam rather than Noah.
2. This is another example in which many people fail to identify the existence of a problem with their own interpretations. Did you notice the two *the*'s in the first and third phrase and the two *a*'s in the second phrase?
3. The inventors of the talking scale seem to have identified real problems that some people face. For example, an advertisement for a talking scale we saw states

   Can't see over your tummy?
   Can't read the numbers way down there?

   However, there may be some situations in which you would not want to use this scale. For example, many people would not want their weight revealed when other people could hear it.
4. The inventors of the sound-activated light switch also identified some problems that this device can help people solve. In particular, it can:

   Hear you coming and turn on the light so you won't come home to a dark house or garage.
   Surprise burglars who enter your house.

   However, the device may not be appropriate for all situations. For example, the light switch will turn off the lights after a short period of time if it does not continue to detect noise. This would probably not be appreciated in a reading room.
5. These are flip-down makeup glasses. They consist of magnifying glasses on hinges so that a person can flip down one side to apply makeup or put on a contact lens while seeing out the other side.

6. This is a new kind of chair designed to allow your body to relax in a position of natural balance. The goal is to help relieve pain in the back, neck, hip joints, and upper legs.

7. Punctuation marks are inventions designed to solve a general problem, namely, that with written language we lose information about pauses and tones of voice that signal questions, exclamations, and so forth. Punctuation marks supply this information in written form.

8. The important role played by punctuation marks can be appreciated by comparing your comprehension of the string of words in the text to the following.

That that is is not that that is not.
Is that it? It is!

9. Part of the difficulty in this problem results from incorrect definitions of the problem. Notice that the problem is not to find the exact spot or time at which the event will occur. The problem, rather, is to show that there is a spot that will be occupied at the same time of day on both trips. Notice that the precise day the trips are made is not especially relevant. One helpful strategy is to imagine that there are actually two monks making this trip on the same day; one monk is walking up the trail, and one monk is walking down the trail. There must be one spot on the trail where the monks meet.

10. This problem requires a careful scheme for representing all the information given. Try forming a table in which each person is represented on the top and side of the table. You can then fill in the table to keep track of which people shook hands with each other. You can start off by arbitrarily assigning numbers to people in the table. After each such assignment, look back and see if any specific conclusions can be drawn. Let H = husband and W = wife.

   1. Let H1 be the person who shook hands with 8 people.
   2. The person who shook hands with 0 people had to be his spouse (W1).
   3. Let H2 be the person who shook hands with 7 people.
   4. Since everyone else shook hands at least twice, W2 had to be the person who shook once.
   5. Let H3 be the person who shook hands with 6 people.
   6. W3 has to be the person who shook hands with 2 people.
   7. Let H4 be the person who shook hands with 5 people.
   8. W4 has to be the person who shook hands with 3 people.
   9. Let H5 be the person who shook hands with 4 people.
  10. W5 had to shake hands with 4 people also.

Since each person the psychologist asked gave a different answer, the only couple whose partners could have shaken hands 4 times each would be the psychologist and his wife (he was the only one we did not have data from). Therefore, his wife shook hands four times.

	Couple 1		Couple 2		Couple 3		Couple 4		Couple 5	
	H1	W1	H2	W2	H3	W3	H4	W4	H5	W5
H1	0	0	X	X	X	X	X	X	X	X
W1	0	0	0	0	0	0	0	0	0	0
H2	X	0	0	0	X	X	X	X	X	X
W2	X	0	0	0	0	0	0	0	0	0
H3	X	0	X	0	0	0	X	X	X	X
W3	X	0	X	0	0	0	0	0	0	0
H4	X	0	X	0	X	0	0	0	X	X
W4	X	0	X	0	X	0	0	0	0	0
H5	X	0	X	0	X	0	X	0	0	0
W5	X	0	X	0	X	0	X	0	0	0

11. This problem can be easily solved by using a strategy of examining specific cases. Try working the problem with specific numbers and various alternative combinations of colored beads into the unknown situations, and you will discover that the answer is yes.

	Red bead jar	Blue bead jar
Assume 50 beads in jar	$50R - 5R = 45R$	$50B + 5R$
Assume 1 red bead is moved back	$45R + (1R + 4B)$	$(50B + 5R) - (1R + 4B)$
Result	$46R + 4B$	$46B + 4R$

12. The problem of understanding Shirley Smith can be facilitated by the availability of conceptual tools, in this case the concept of "social comparison." Theories of social comparison suggest that many judgments we make (about our talents, wealth, achievement, and so on) are not based on absolute standards. Instead, they are based on comparisons with others. When compared to other students in married housing, the Smiths seemed no worse off than anyone else. Once they moved to an affluent suburb, however, there were many instances in which others were considerably more wealthy than they were; hence, Mrs. Smith felt economically deprived.*

*From M. Mark and T. Cook. Relative deprivation: When does it lead to anger, achievement or disengagement? *Alternatives—Perspectives on Society and Environment, 8,* 13–17, 1979.

13. Most people have a difficult time solving this problem. The average response is that the paper will extend 1 or 2 feet after 50 folds. With the help of a systematic analysis of each step plus some mathematical tools, it becomes clear that these answers are way off the mark.

Consider the following calculations. If the paper is originally 0.001 inches thick, it is 2 times as thick after one folding (2×0.001). When the paper is folded a second time, it again becomes twice as thick, which is 4 times the original thickness, that is, $2 \times 2\ (0.001)$ inches thick, or $2^2\ (0.001)$. When it is folded for a third time it is 8 times as thick as the original, or $2^3\ (0.001)$—this is double the thickness for the second fold. Similarly, the fourth fold is $2^4\ (0.001)$ times as thick as the original. Thus, 50 folds of the tissue paper would equal $2^{50}\ (0.001)$, which is about 17,770,000 miles. This is considerably larger than the 2 or 3 feet of thickness most people estimate. Indeed, it is over one-fourth the distance from Venus to the Earth.

14. This problem also involves a systematic analysis of what happens at each step in the problem (e.g., fish 1 eats two 2s for a total of two 2s, each 2 eats two 3s for a total of four 3s, each 3 eats two 4s for a total of eight 4s, and so on. We can therefore see the beginning of a geometric progression (2, 4, 8, . . .). The availability of mathematical tools makes it much easier to solve this problem. The formula is 2^6, for a total of 64 size 7 fish that must be eaten each day.

Incidentally, it is this progression in the food chain that causes what has been called "biological magnification." Even a small percentage of toxins in a lake can become amplified in concentration in larger fish because they eat the equivalent of a large number of small fish each day.

15. When the robot is seen in context, some of its design flaws become more apparent. For example, its sponges are too big to be dipped into its head (the bucket). Furthermore, since the arms do not bend, the robot will push itself off the building if it lowers its arms much more.

    Information gleaned from observing things in context is analogous to acting on the basis of some idea or invention and then looking at the effects. If we ignore the <u>act</u> and <u>look</u> components of problem solving we will frequently fail to spot flaws in our ideas. Ideally, we want to spot these through imagination or through the use of prototypes so that we can correct them as soon as possible and with the least amount of expense.

16. The common answer to this problem is 5. However, if you imagine explicitly performing the *activity* of making and smoking the cigars and *looking* at the effects, you will see that the correct answer is 6. The man can make one additional cigar from the butts of the other 5 cigars.

Chapter 3

1. How many stops did the bus make? Most people are not prepared for this question. They anticipated a different question; namely, how many people were left on the bus? Different strategies are necessary to prepare for these different questions. This is a good illustration of how various strategies may or may not be most appropriate depending on the memory problem one is attempting to solve.

    What was the name of the bus driver? Most people have a difficult time answering this question from memory because they cannot remember being told about anyone's name. If you look back at the first sentence of the passage, you will see that the answer to this question is quite familiar to you.

2. An acrostic for remembering the cranial nerves that has been around for some time is: "On old Olympus' towering tops a Finn and German vend some hops."

3. A helpful acrostic for remembering whether to set one's clock forward or back an hour is, "Spring forward and fall back."

4. You could combine the rhyme peg word system (one is a bun, two is a shoe, and so on) and an acrostic in the following manner. Think of the acrostic, "You must wear two shoes to get in the door and stand in line,". . . . From the peg word system you know that "two is a shoe," so two shoes equals 22. Similarly, you know from the peg word system that "four is a door" (so, door helps you remember the number 4) and that "nine is a line" (so, line helps you remember 9).

5. You could use acrostics, such as "fir is smooth" and "a rough hem stands out." For the latter, think of "hem" as short for hemlock and think of "standing out" as illustrating a rough twig.

6. For "across," an example using acrostics is, "You only cross the gate to heaven once." Let "across" remind you of "cross" and let "once" remind you of the number of *c*'s.

7. For "facilitate," you might state to yourself that, "The face of a penny has one picture of Lincoln." Let facilitate remind you of "face" and let the thought of one picture of Lincoln (which begins with an *l*) remind you that there is only one *l*.

8. For "development," you might think, "When you want to develop film, people should *not* enter the darkroom while the process is going on." Let "development" remind you of develop (as in develop the film) and let "do not enter" remind you of "no *e*" after develop.

9. You might imagine someone climbing a big hill (for the first part of his last name) and use the sound of last part of his name (Hillary—*e*) to signify Everest.

10. One possibility is to let the "bert" part of Hubert remind you of dirt and the "Booth" remind you of boots. Dirt left by boots needs to be removed, preferably by a vacuum cleaner.

11. You could let the "rank" in Frank remind you of rank, let the middle initial (*t*) remind you of "tops," and let the *c* in Cary remind you of computers. Thinking about "ranks tops in computer sales" could then help you remember his position in IBM (assuming that you are familiar with the fact that IBM is a leader in sales of computers).

12. For Harriet Eisely you might let her flowing hair remind you of Harriet and her distinctive eyes remind you of Eiseley.

13. For Lynn Foreman you might let his big chin remind you of Lynn (they rhyme) and let his big forehead remind you of Foreman.

14. For Rose Lipman you could let her round face remind you of something like "ring around the rosey" and her thin lips remind you of Lipman.

Chapter 4

Possible answers include:

1. Spider web
2. Lawn sprinkler
3. Parking meter
4. Dirty window

Some possible answers are:

5. Thermal underwear
6. The inside story
7. 4 degrees below zero
8. Reading between the lines
9. A terrible spell of weather
10. As noted in the text, people need to make inferences to comprehend. If they lack the background knowledge, it must be supplied.

    The instructions could be improved if they clarified such things as the need to insert the pencil in the hole, how much pressure to apply to the pencil, how long to continue cranking, and what to use as a reference in determining the clockwise direction.

    For people who have never used a pencil, it might also be necessary to clarify the purpose of the pencil sharpener, the time it will take to perform the operation, which end of the pencil to insert, and what the finished product will look like.

11. One way to help children understand the significance of the previous facts about camels is to help them see how these features permit camels to survive in deserts. One aspect of deserts is sudden, severe sandstorms that can have adverse effects on the eyes, nose, and ears. Camels' eyelids, nose passages, and ear openings have evolved as protection against sandstorms.

12. Children who understand the significance of these characteristics of camels should be better able to understand additional events, such as a description of people traveling across a desert who wear veils over their faces despite the heat.

13. Many people miss this problem because they fail to gain access to knowledge that is potentially available to them.

   The most common mistake is to assume that the spy begins drilling inside the *left cover of the book on the left* and that he continues drilling until he reaches the *right-most cover of the book on the right*. People who make this mistake have usually failed to mentally imagine picking up the first book, opening it, and starting to read on the first page. *The first page is on the right of the first book.* Similarly, the last page of the second book is on its left. The hole drilled by the spy therefore goes only through two book covers (each ¼ inch thick) for a total of ½ inch.

   This example illustrates a common problem. We often fail to spontaneously gain access to relevant information (such as, where the first and last pages in a book are found). Once we are prompted to use this information, our errors often seem obvious. The IDEAL problem solver constantly works to minimize such access errors.

Chapter 5

1. This statement encourages the reader to make many inferences, but what it actually means could be quite different from those invited inferences. For example, it could mean that nine of ten doctors surveyed have at one time or another recommended this product to at least one person (not necessarily a patient and not necessarily to the exclusion of other similar products). It does not necessarily mean that the doctors prefer this product or advise patients to use it more than any other product. Try to think of some unusual products or substances that could legitimately fit this claim.

2. Assuming that all the children were of a comparable age and received comparable achievement tests, we would still want to have additional information, especially about the samples of students who were tested. Was the average score for American children lowest simply because all American children are encouraged to go to school, even those who are not interested, whereas other countries may not include such children in the sample who took the test? Some data relevant to this question would be whether the best American students (the top one-third) did as well as the best in other countries. This would say something about whether the average scores say more about sampling than about the quality of instruction students receive.

3. There are a number of possible problems with this statement. One reason for higher incomes is that the first school may teach courses (like business) that usually result in higher salaries than those taught by the second school (like education).

   A second reason may be that the first university may have been in operation much longer; hence, its graduates have had time to earn higher salaries because of their seniority.

   A third reason is that the first university may attract better students in the first place. They may graduate and earn more only because they began at a higher level, not because the instructional program is inherently better.

4. The relationship between grades and computers is correlational. Computers at home could contribute to better grades, but it is also possible that students who get better grades are more likely to take an interest in computers or that parents who take an active role in stimulating their child's intellectual development influence their children to perform better in school and are more likely to buy home computers to improve the learning environment at home. If the school board wanted to know if computers at home actually influenced performance at school, they would need to conduct a controlled experiment. (See Chapter 5 for discussions of experimental design.)

5. This finding is part of a series of investigations known as the Hawthorne studies, which were conducted at the Western Electric Hawthorne plant. The findings are indicative of what some have labeled the Hawthorne effect. In these investigations worker productivity seemed to improve regardless of the illumination level under which workers operated. For example, in one experiment the lighting was *reduced* to the intensity of ordinary moonlight and subjects still maintained their production level. In another study, when light bulbs were replaced with bulbs of the same intensity, subjects reported that they liked the increased illumination. These results are often used to illustrate the effects management can have on worker productivity when workers think management is taking an increased interest in their problems.

6. No. None of the men who love strawberry pie live on Gorky Street. See the diagram below.

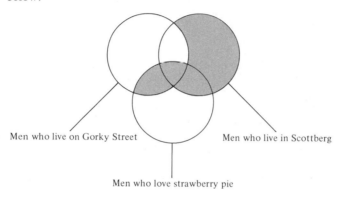

Men who live on Gorky Street   Men who live in Scottberg

Men who love strawberry pie

(Shaded areas denote no members.)

7. No. It is possible that some xenos are not red. See the diagram below.

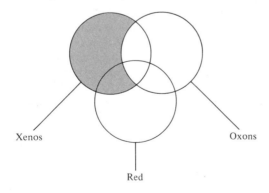

Xenos   Oxons

Red

(Shaded areas denote no members.)

8. Yes. See the diagram below.

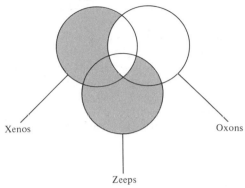

(Shaded areas denote no members.)

9. No. I may have skipped the party yet still failed to do my homework. The form of reasoning being used here is: If A (go to party), then B (cannot do my homework). If one were to reason "B, therefore A," one would be commiting the fallacy of affirming the consequent.

10. Although the form of logical reasoning that leads to such a conclusion is valid, this is a clear case in which one is testing not only a theory but also additional assumptions that relate that theory to observable data. For example, it is possible that the theory is correct and yet injections of RNA will have no immediate effect on memory. It is also possible that the site of the injection could be an important determinant of the effect observed, that the injection must be given several days in advance, and so forth.

11. This game will have no winner because players will quickly encounter a situation in which neither player can advance without breaking the rule of never occupying the same square simultaneously.

12. The first step is to define the problem. What information is being requested: Is the problem to differentiate the liar from the one who is truthful or simply to obtain correct directions? In the first problem the task is to obtain correct directions. Since only one question can be asked, the problem really becomes, "What question will the liar and one who is truthful both answer correctly?" Lying is negating the truth, so one might think about situations in which negation or negatives can be eliminated. For example, in grammar a double negative is really a positive, or in mathematics if you multiply two negative numbers you get a positive number. To use a similar strategy in this problem, we would need to ask a question that required the liar to lie twice. One way to do this is to ask a question that requires the person to answer how they would answer, for example, "If I asked you if this was the correct path would you say yes?"

13. In the second problem the task is really to differentiate the liar from the brother who tells the truth or to formulate a question that each will answer differently. This problem is related to the previous example in that it involves a double negative—the liar lies but is always misinformed—so the answer is correct. When will the two brothers answer questions differently? Since both the truthful brother and the liar will give an answer that is usually correct, all we need to do is to ask either of them about themselves or the other brother. For example, if asked, "Are you a liar?", the truthful brother would say no. The liar would think he wasn't a liar but would lie about it and say "yes." A question such as, "Is your brother a liar?" will produce similar results.

Chapter 6

1. Most people generate such items as a magnifying glass, an underwater sound amplifier, or an underwater light. These are all fine answers, but it is nevertheless useful to ask whether they are constrained by various implicit assumptions.

    Most people generate inventions designed to help people enjoy actual fish that live in an aquarium; they therefore make an implicit assumption that is unnecessary. The problem of helping people enjoy the sights and sounds of tropical fish in their own homes could also be solved by inventing an aquarium videotape. In fact, such tapes are on the market and can be bought in many video stores.

2. The men did not play one another. The assumption that they *did* play one another renders the problem insolvable.

3. The simplest solution is to pick up the second glass from the left and pour the water from it into the next to last glass on the right. Many people fail to generate this solution because they make the implicit assumption that the water cannot be poured from one glass into another.

4. Most people generate such reasons as

    Wants the exercise.
    Needs the exercise.
    Wants to surprise you.
    Wants to visit someone on the way.
    The elevator is broken.

    These all involve assumptions that the cousin is essentially normal. An alternate possibility is that the cousin is so short he cannot reach the higher buttons. He therefore punches the highest button he can reach and walks from there.

5. The most obvious solution to this problem is the one least frequently generated. Simply throw the ball straight up in the air. It will stop and eventually reverse its direction.

6. The most common error with this problem is to assume one is dealing with Roman numerals. If you think of the numbers as Arabic numerals, the answer is simple: six.

7. The most common error on this problem is to make the assumption that you must stay within the imaginary lines that form the square. The solution illustrated below goes outside these imaginary lines.

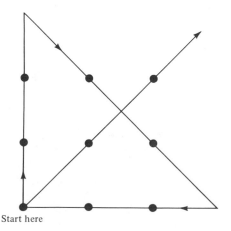

Start here

8. This problem is similar to the classic nine-dot problem in that people tend to make assumptions that are not necessarily true and that make a solution impossible. In this case most people make the assumption that the tire tracks were produced by a car. The only reason the sheriff knew which man he wanted was because the tire tracks were produced by a wheelchair and the man sitting in the middle of the porch was in a wheelchair.*

9. A seeming inconsistency in the passage is that the man took off his overcoat, yet the passage said it was cold and dark. At first glance this appears to be an illogical thing to do.

    Imagine that we make the assumption that the car had fallen into a lake ("his submerged car came to a halt . . ."). Now, the apparent inconsistency between the cold temperature and the act of removing the coat is resolved.

*Personal communication, Joe Hatcher.

AUTHOR INDEX

SUBJECT INDEX